I0846312

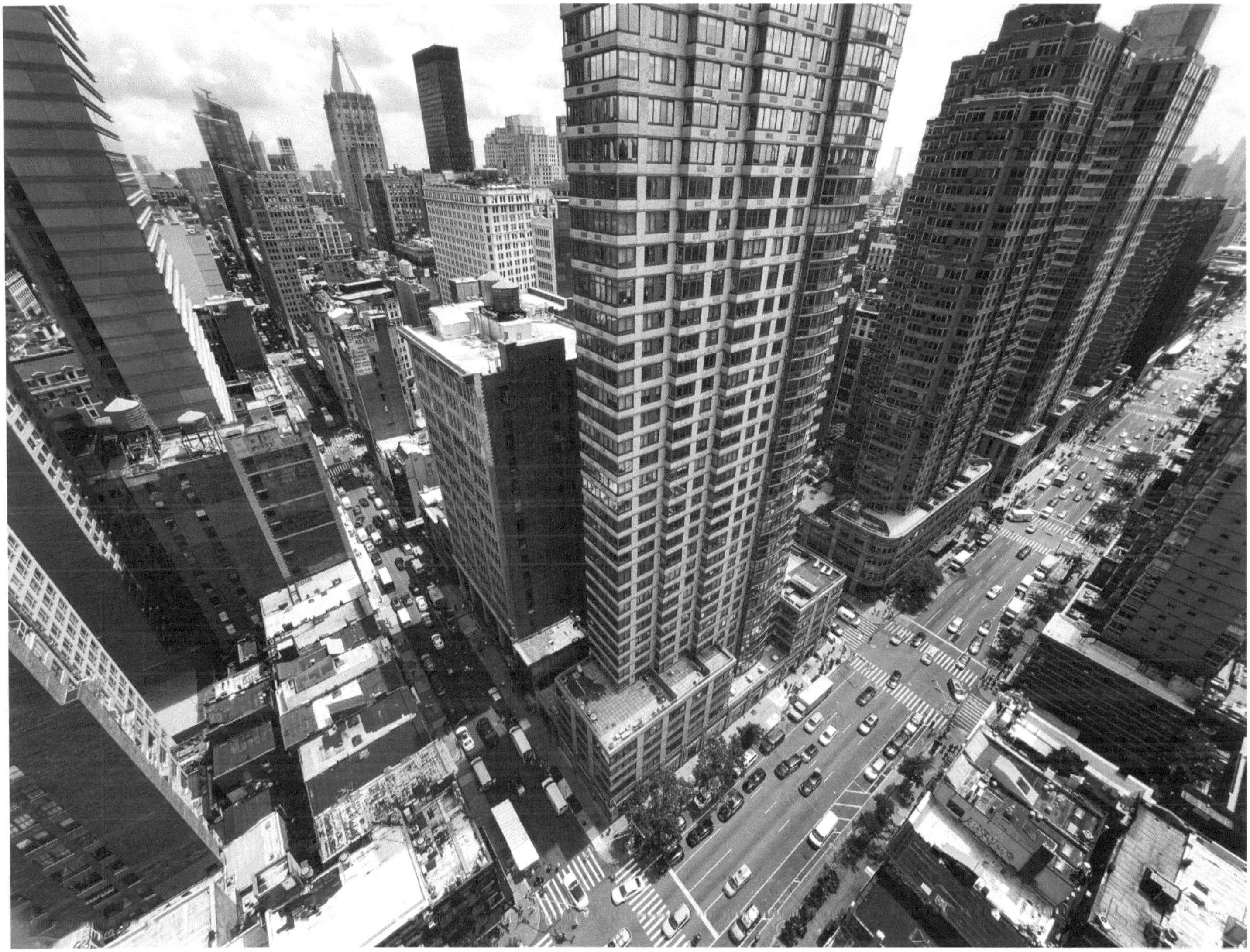

Dedication

For my parents who have given me everything.

Acknowledgement

First and foremost, I extend my deepest gratitude to my parents…again. Their unwavering love has been the roots from which I've grown. Every picture holds a story, and behind each story, there's a hint of their influence.

Friends and family, your support has shaped this collection into a tapestry of cherished memories. Every image here is a testament to the community that has uplifted and inspired me. For always believing in the vision behind my lens, thank you.

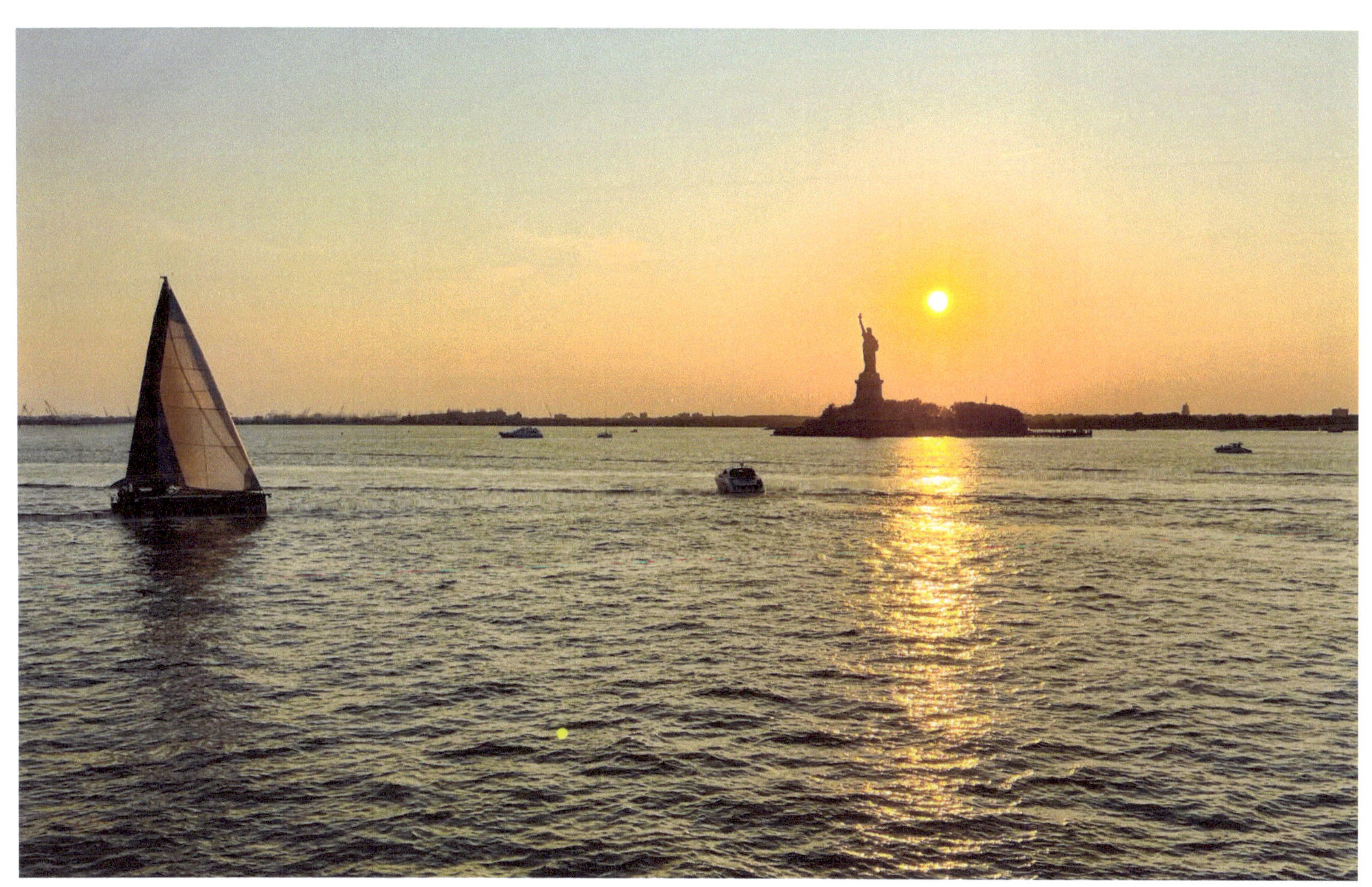

Hope

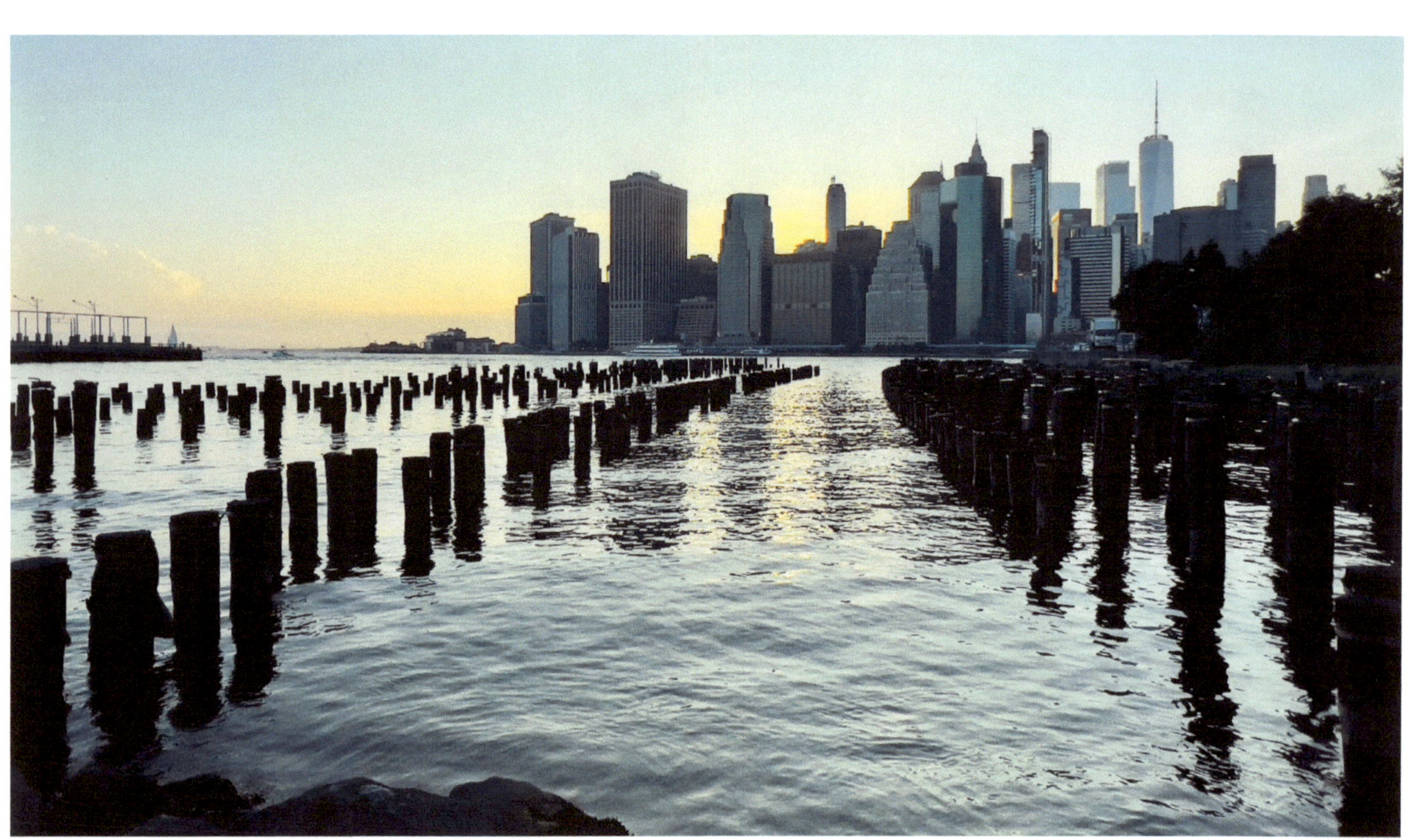

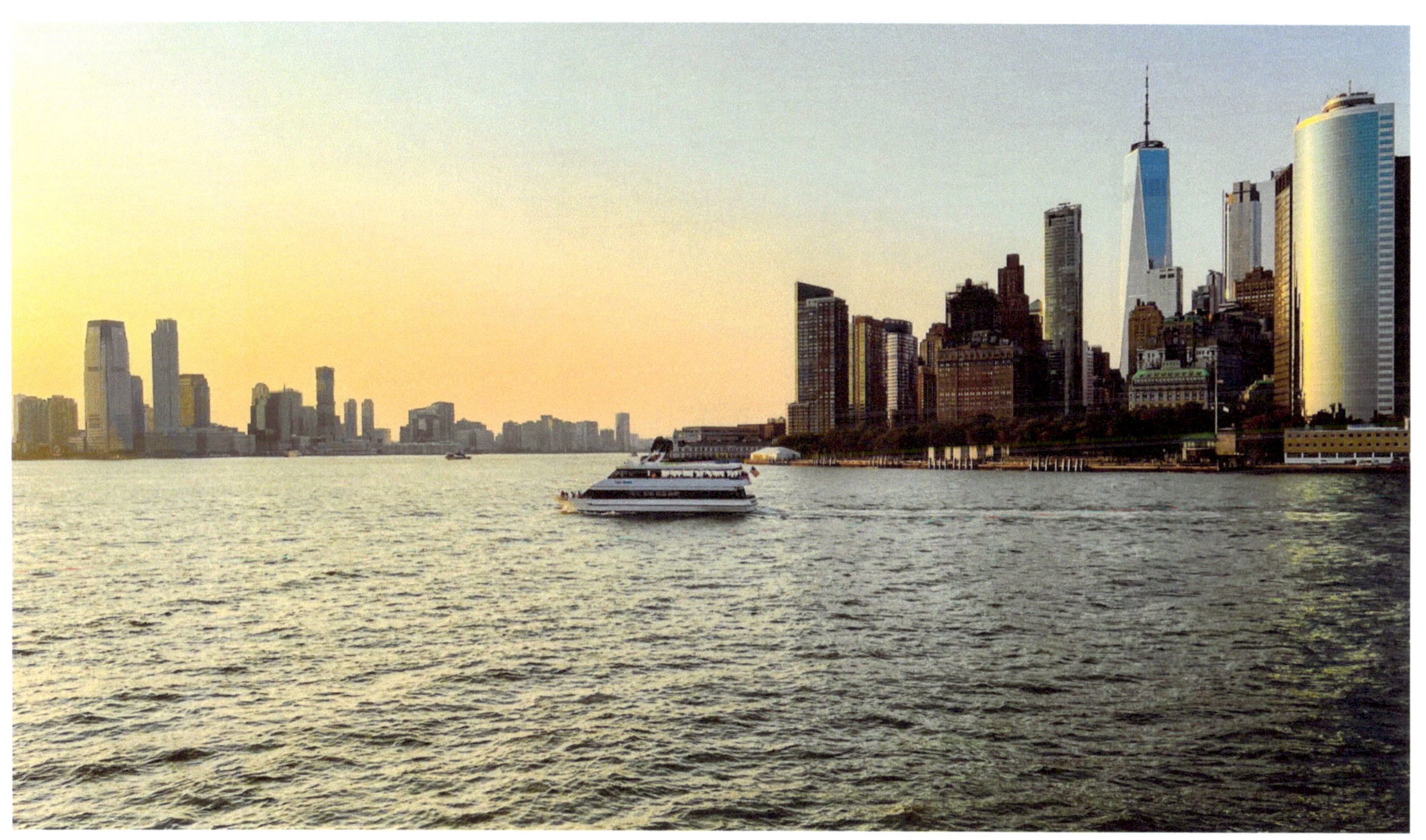

Gilded

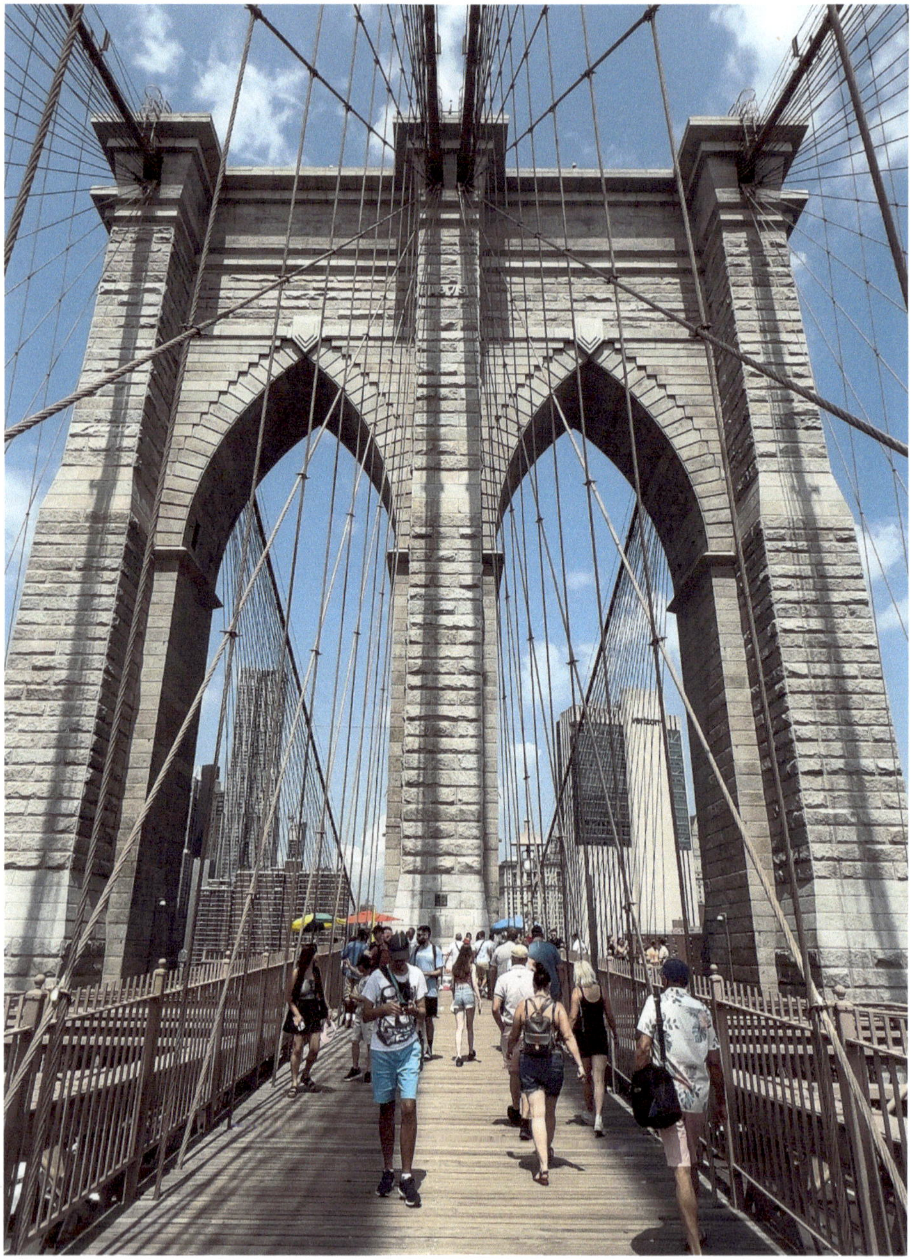

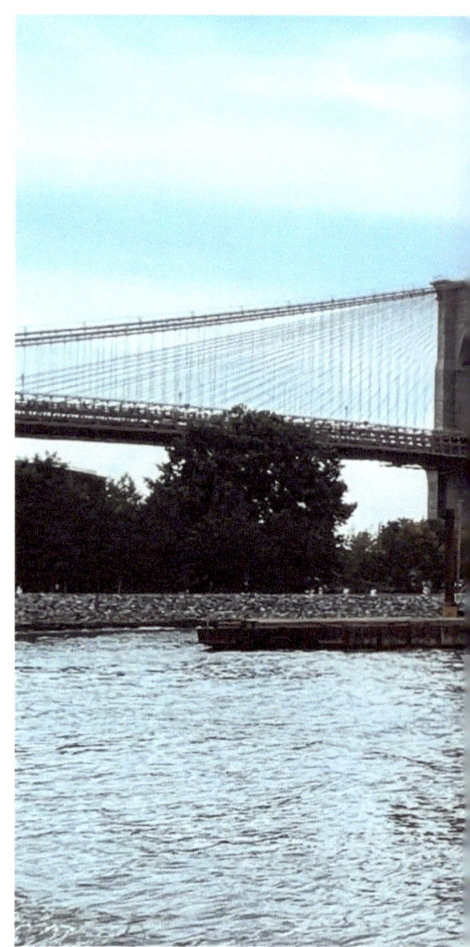

Walk The Brooklyn Bridge

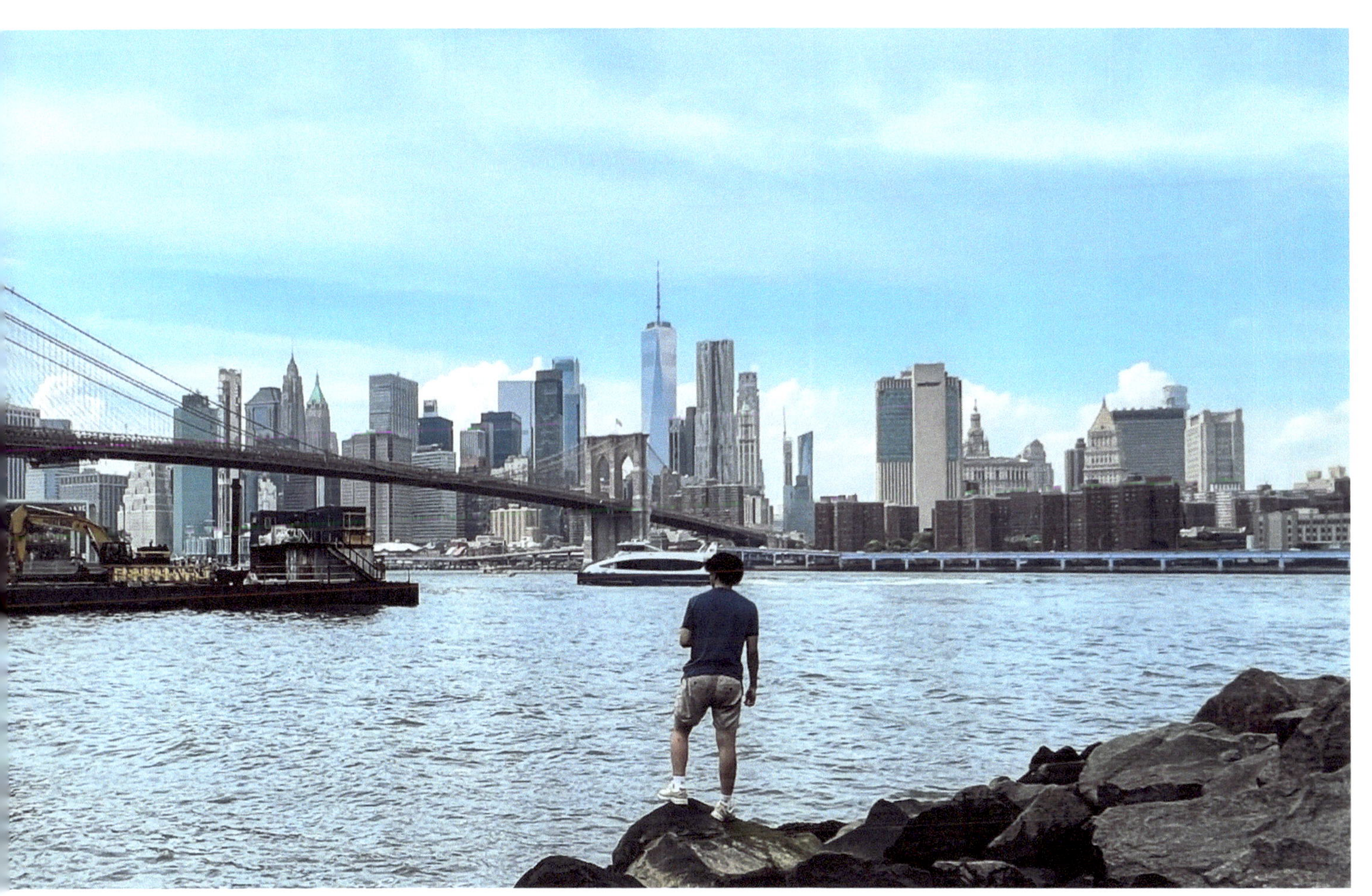

Dream

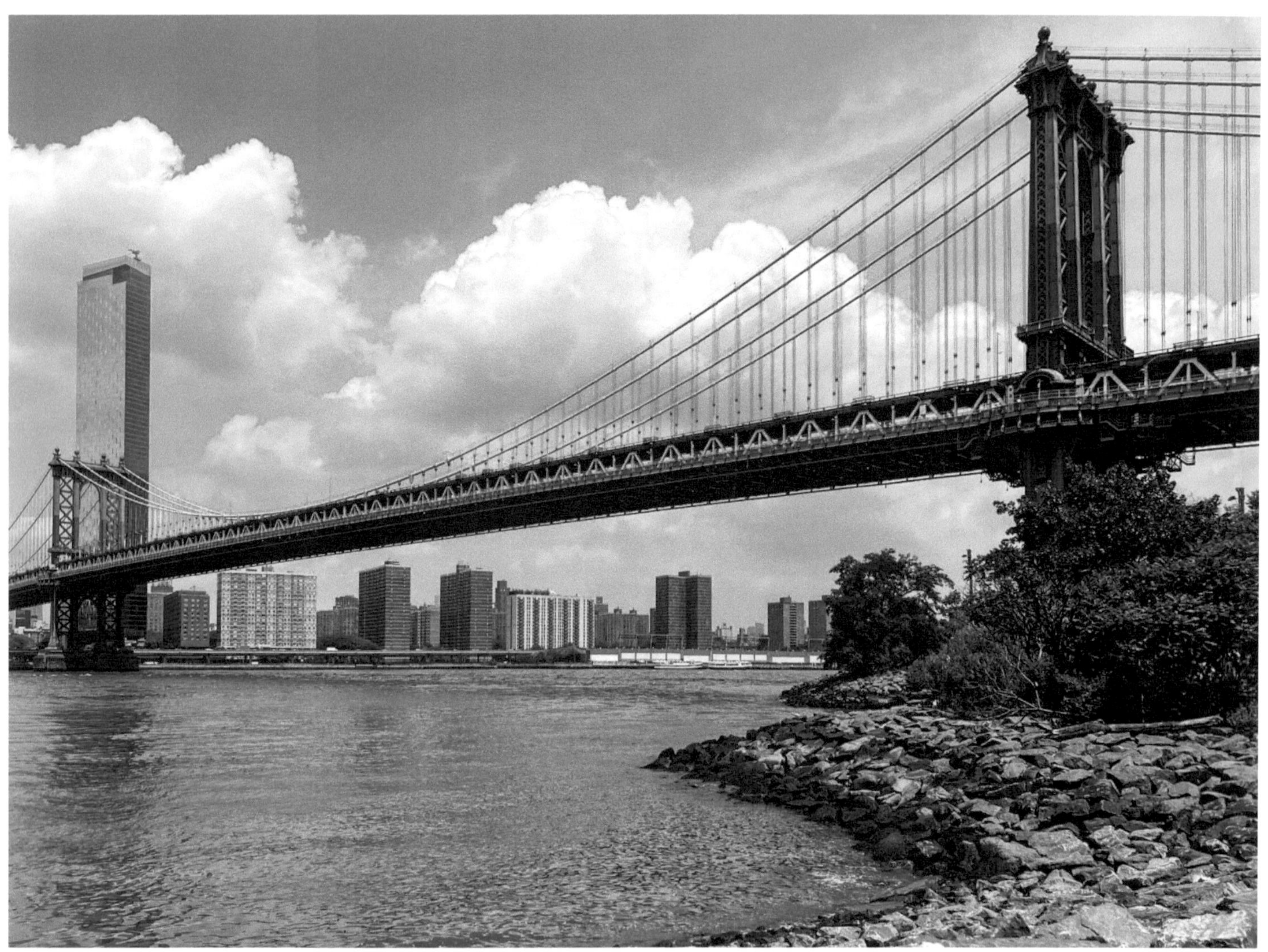

Iconic

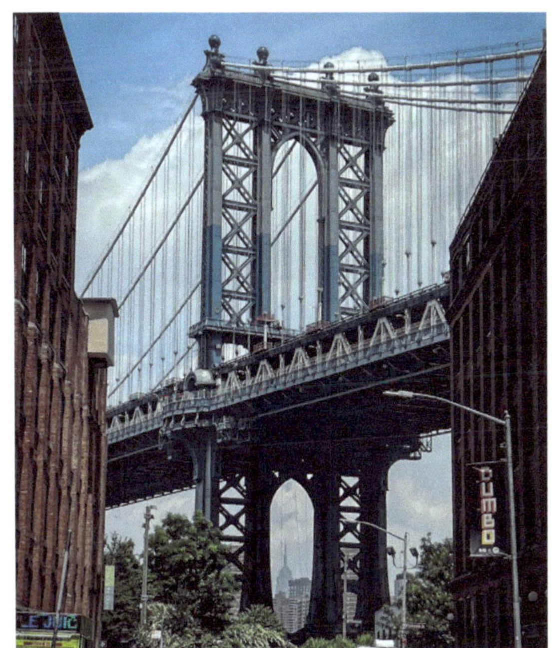

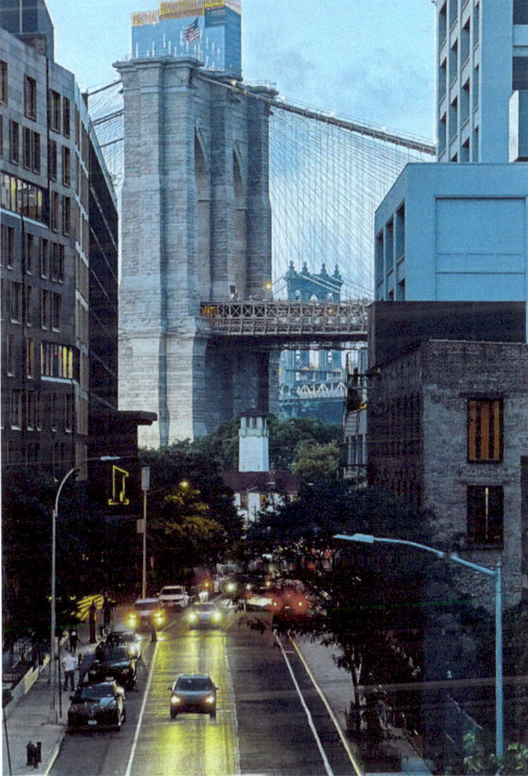

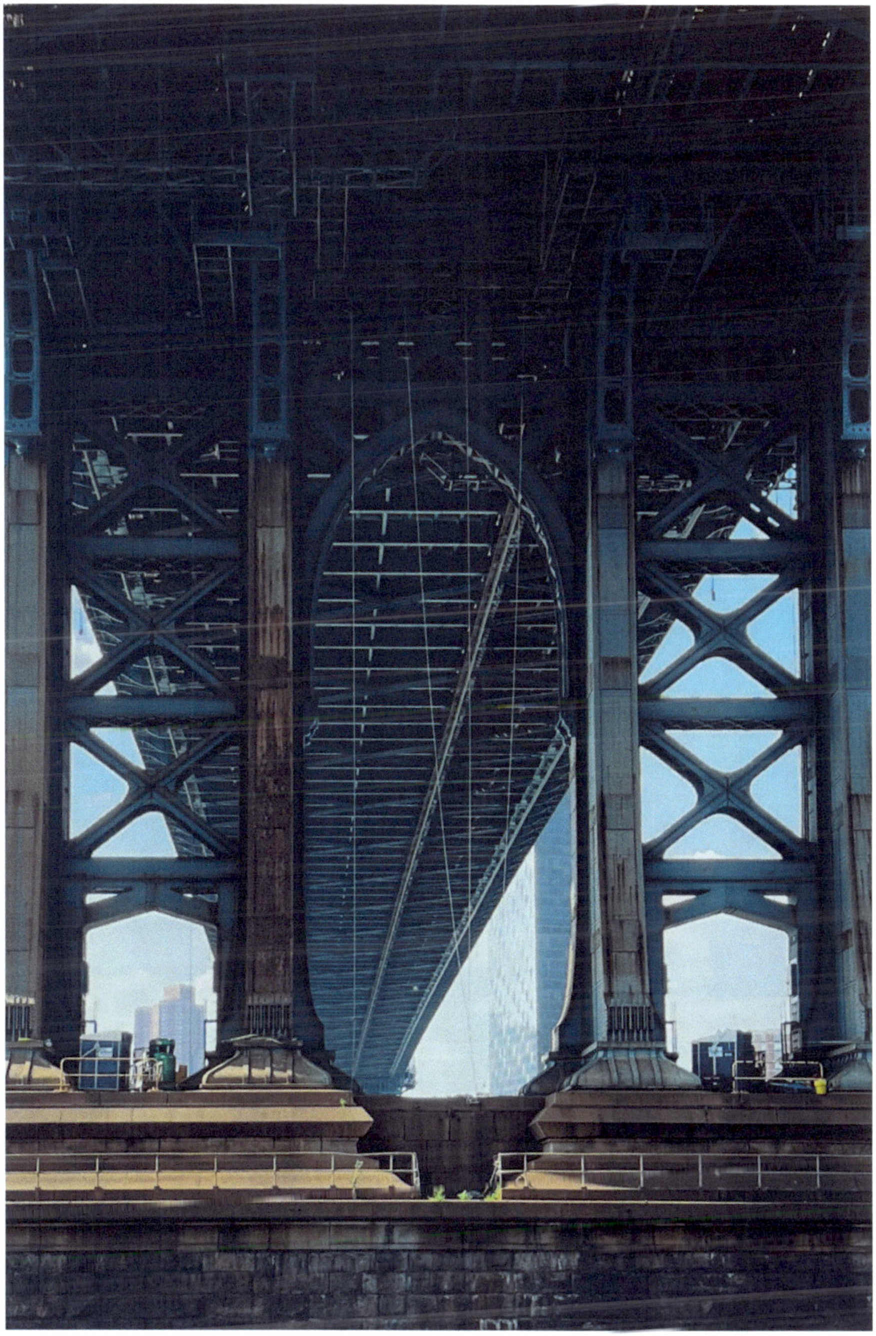

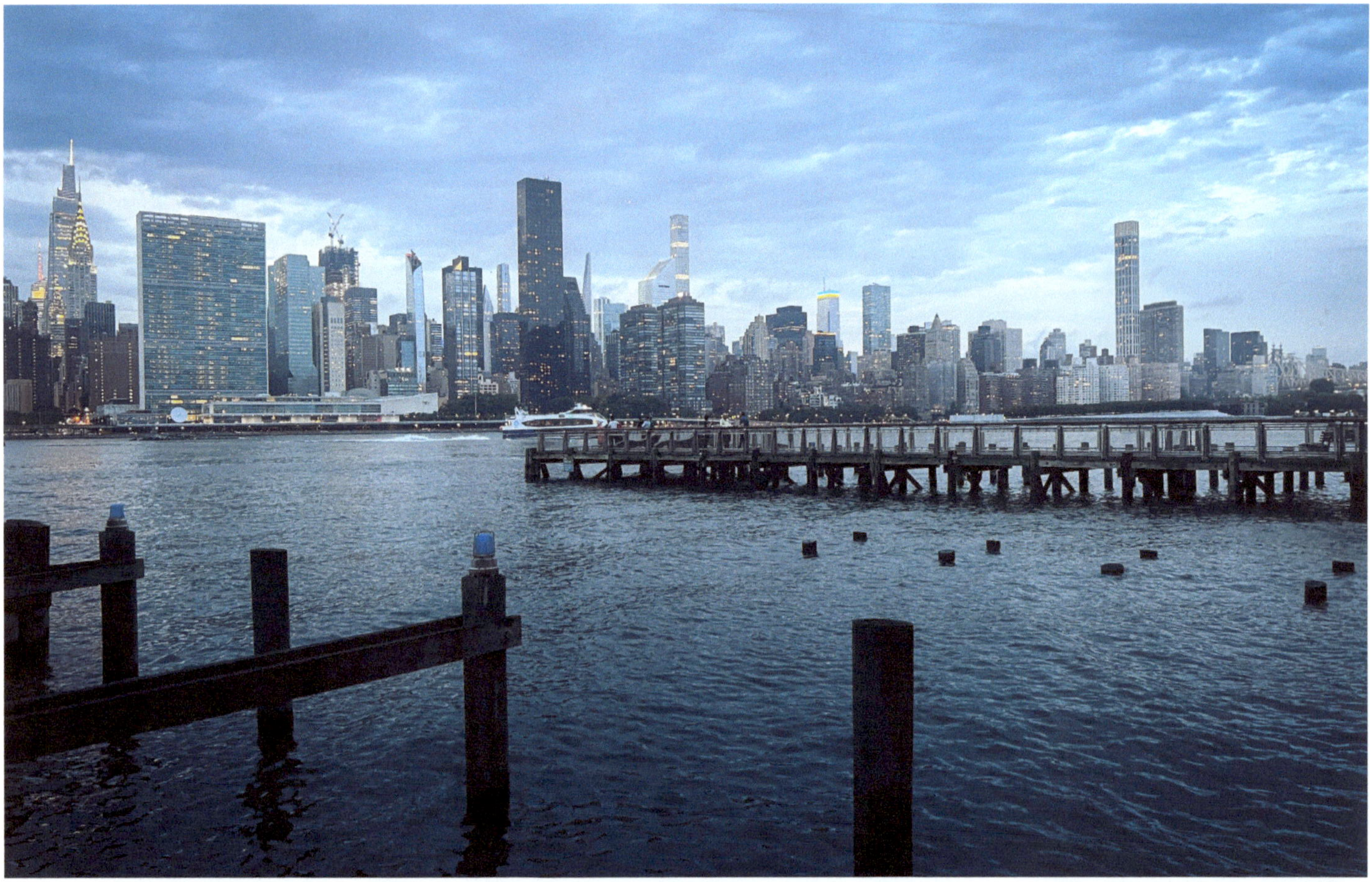

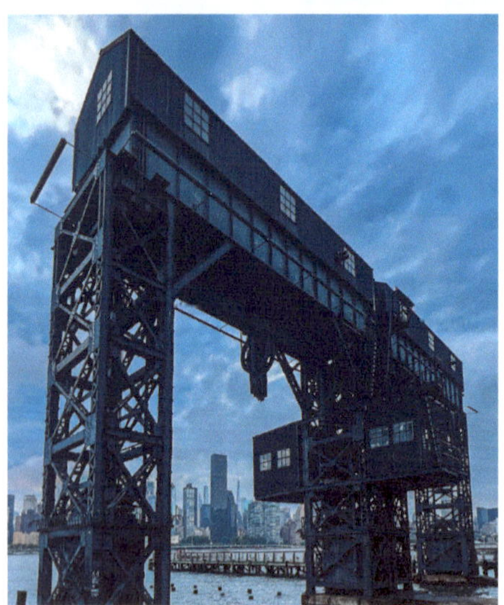

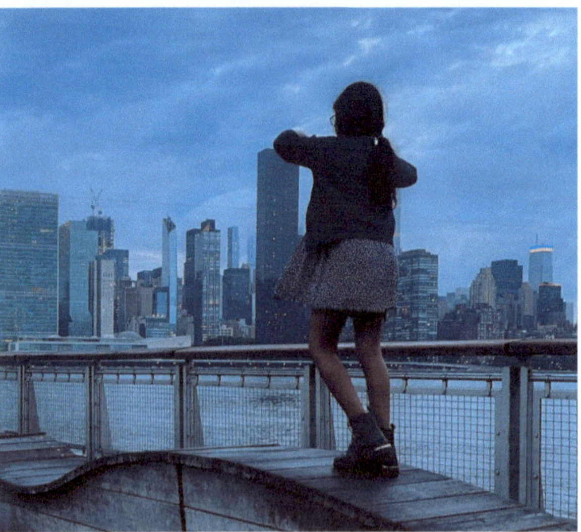

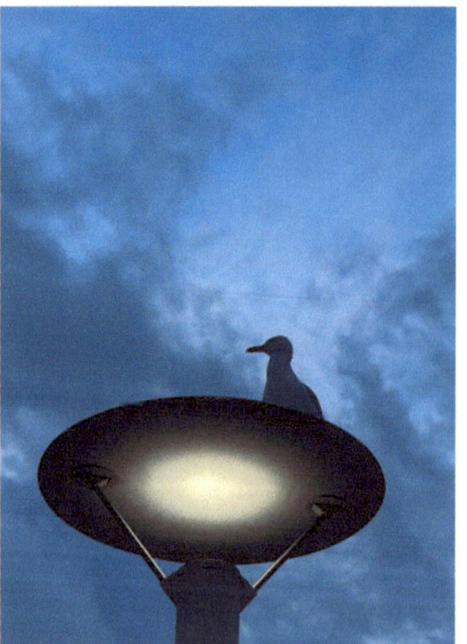

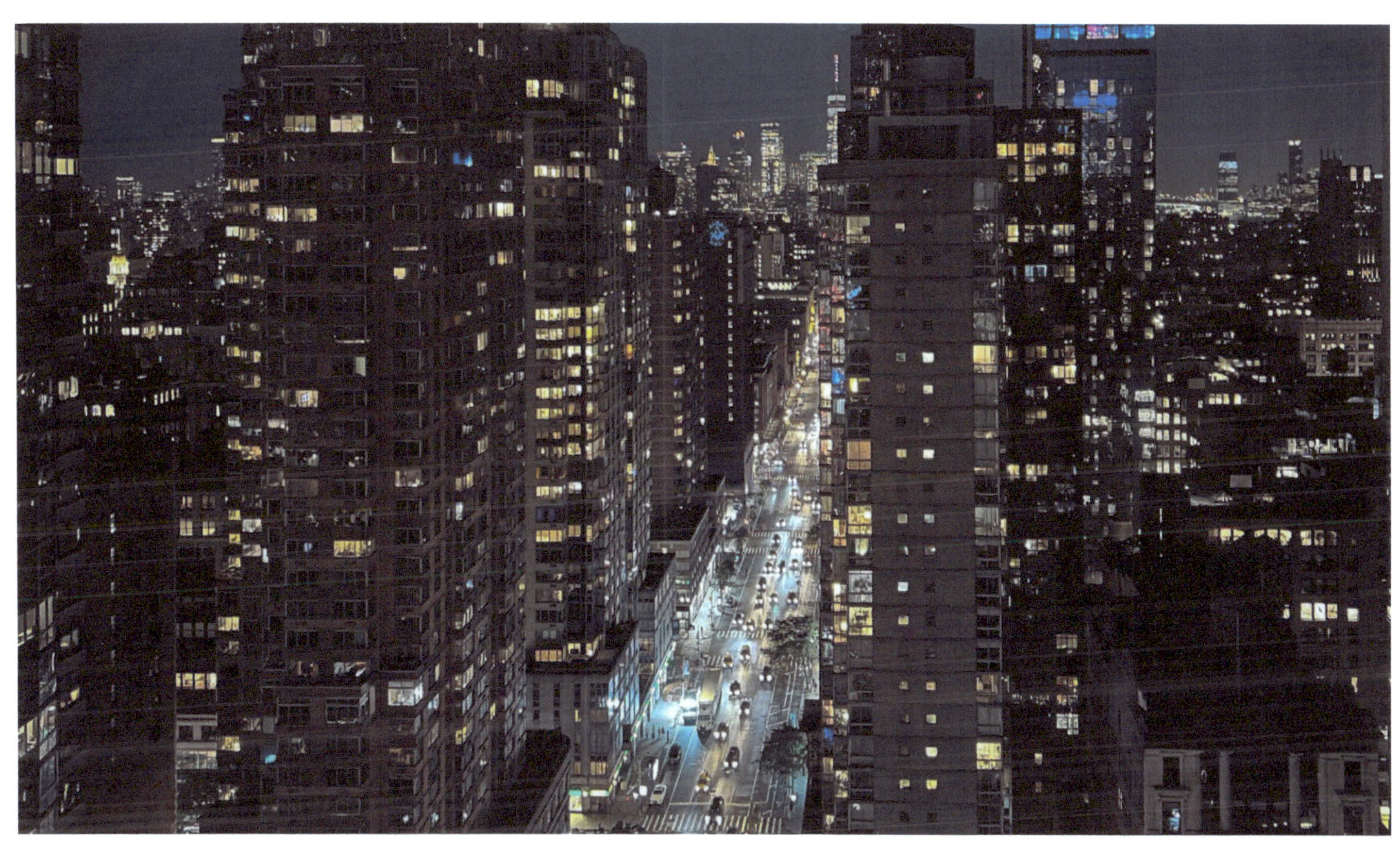

Blue Motley   Night Owl

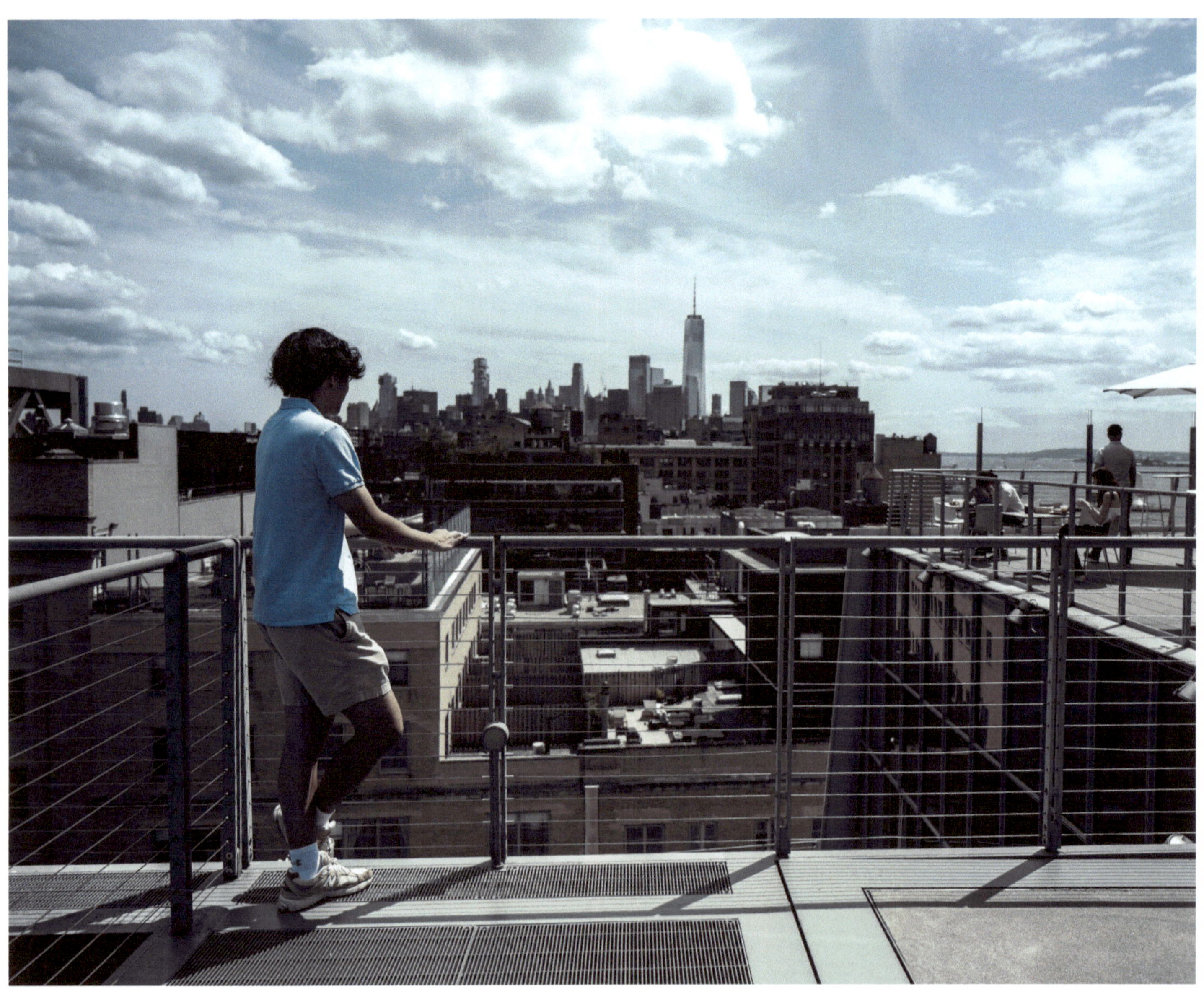

On The Urban Stage

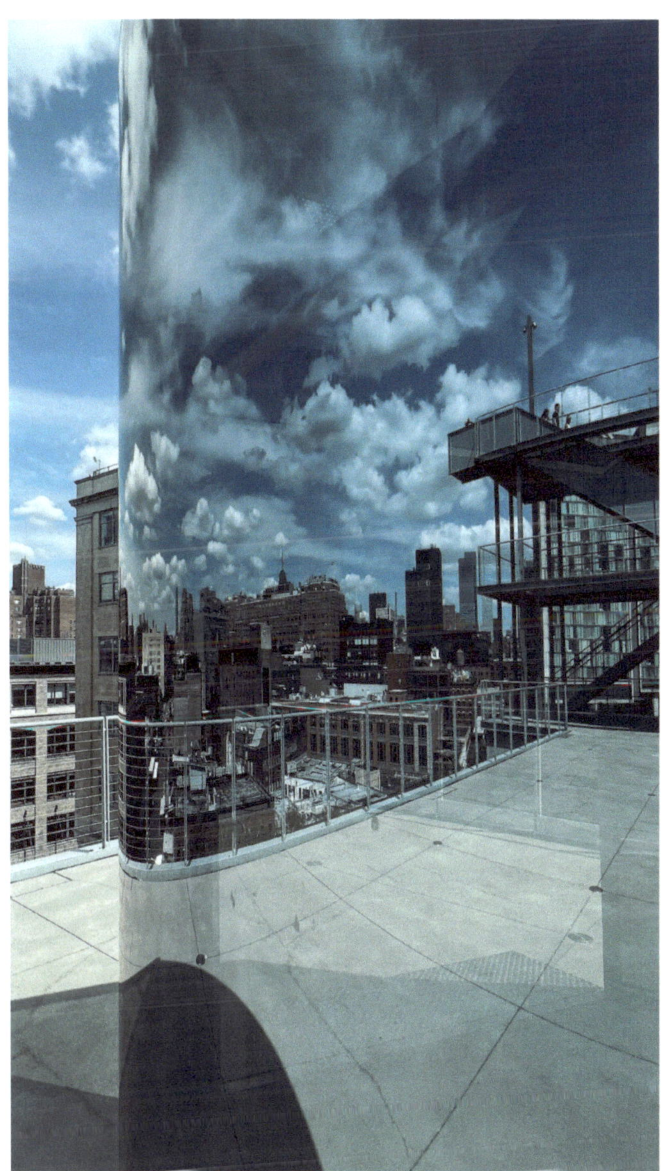
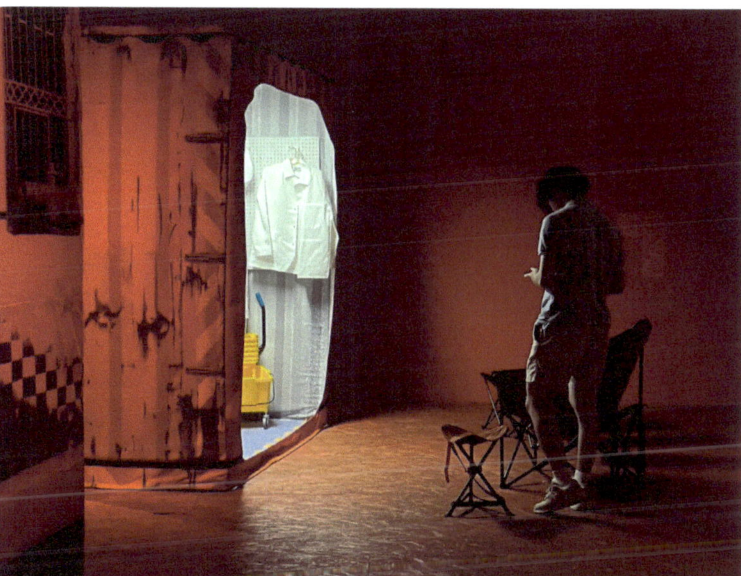
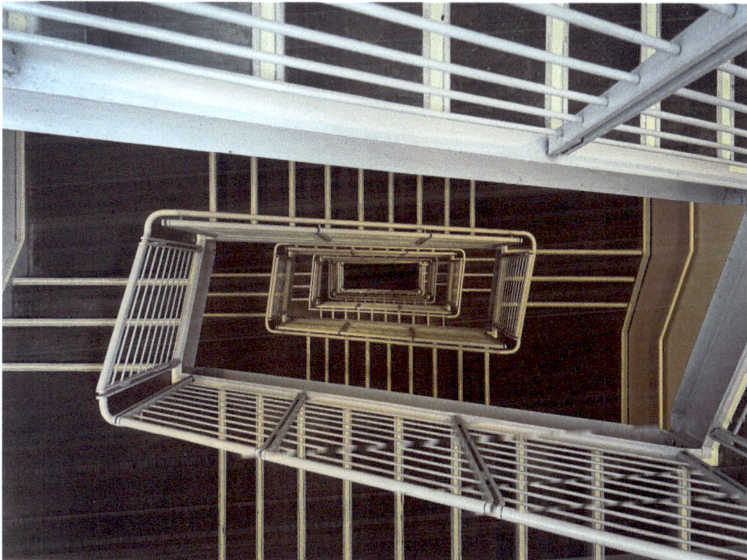

Whitney Museum

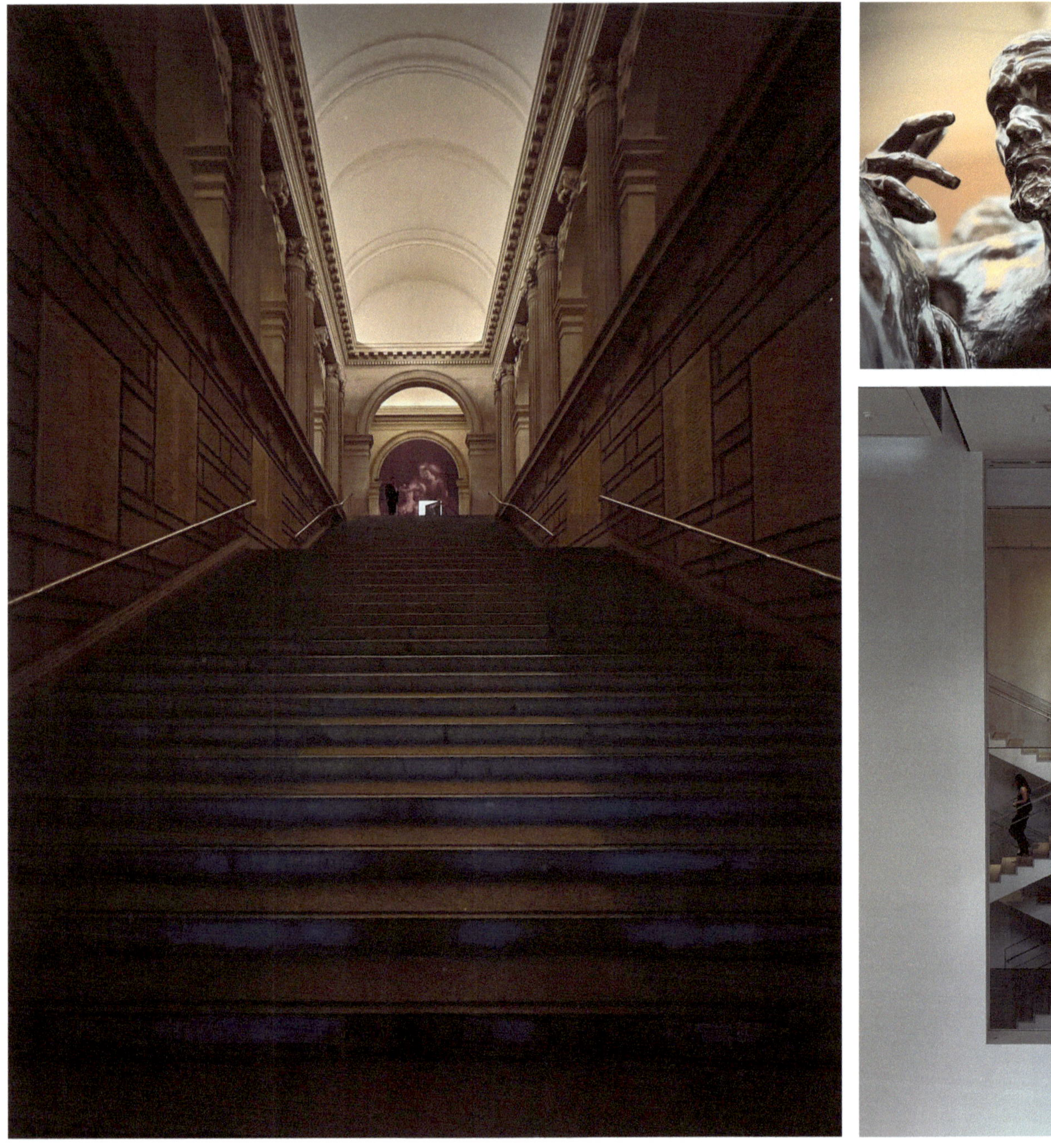

Fresh Eyes

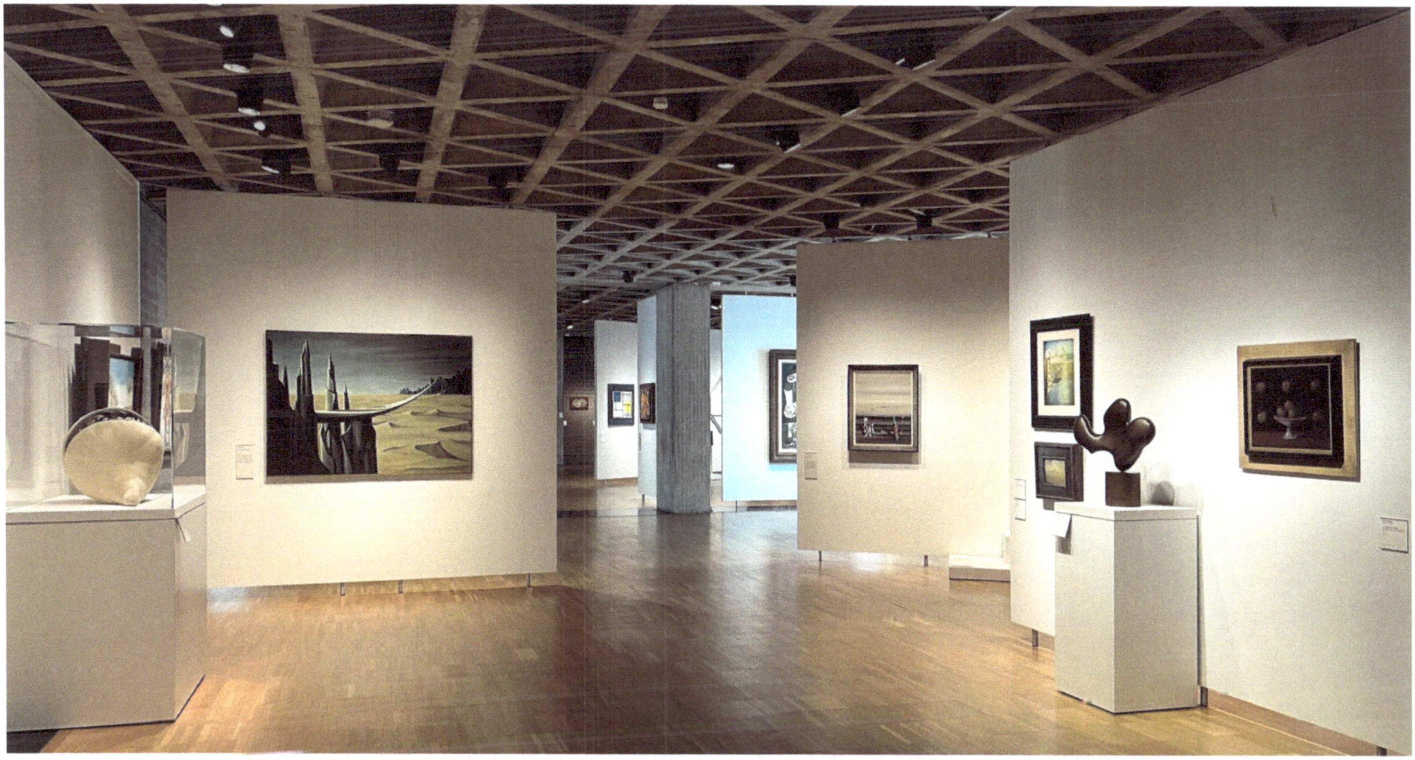

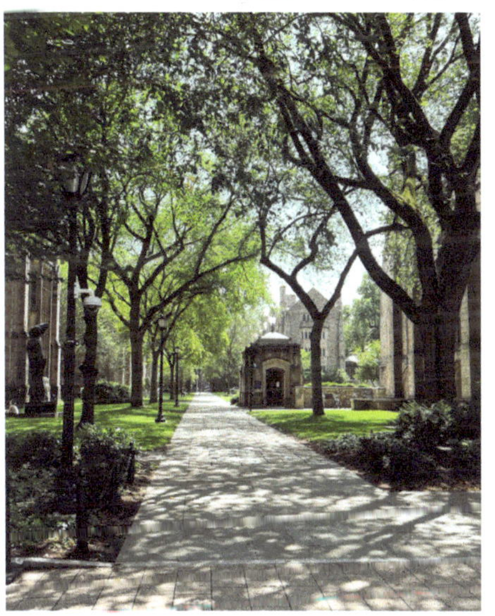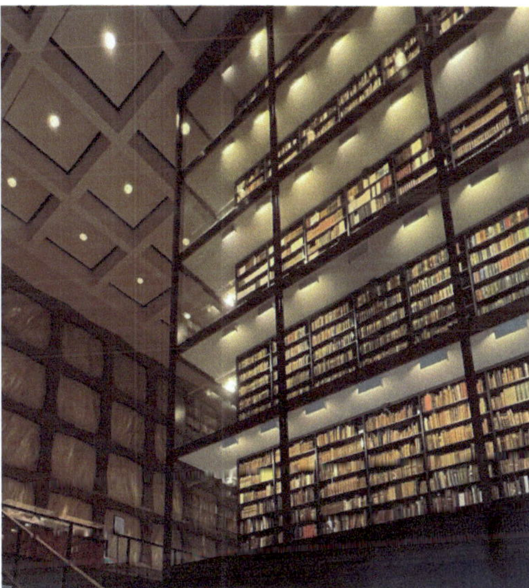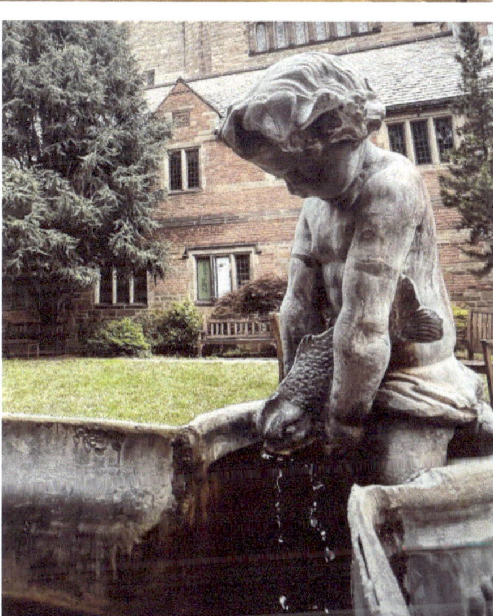

Yale Campus Encounters

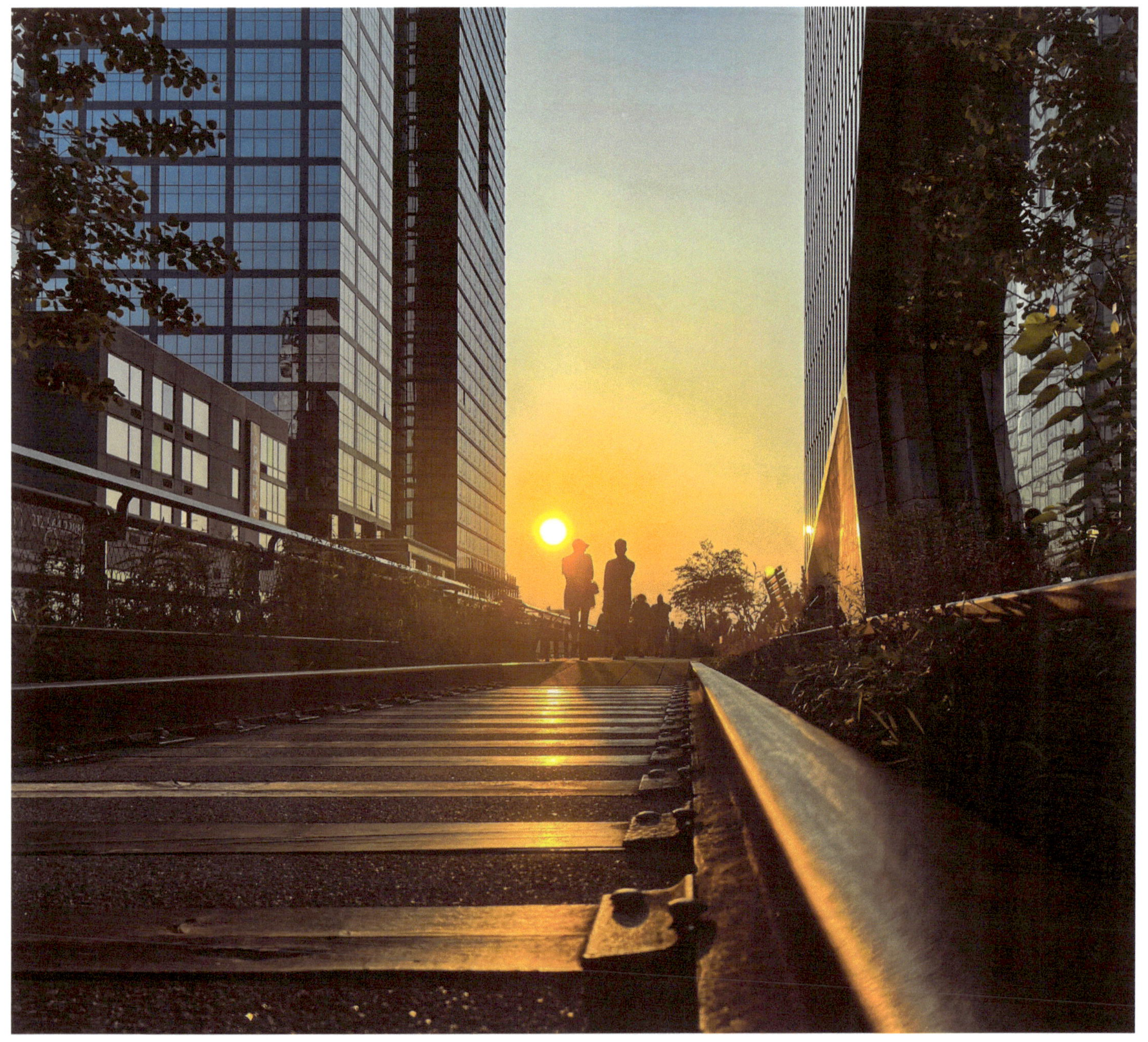

Living The High Line

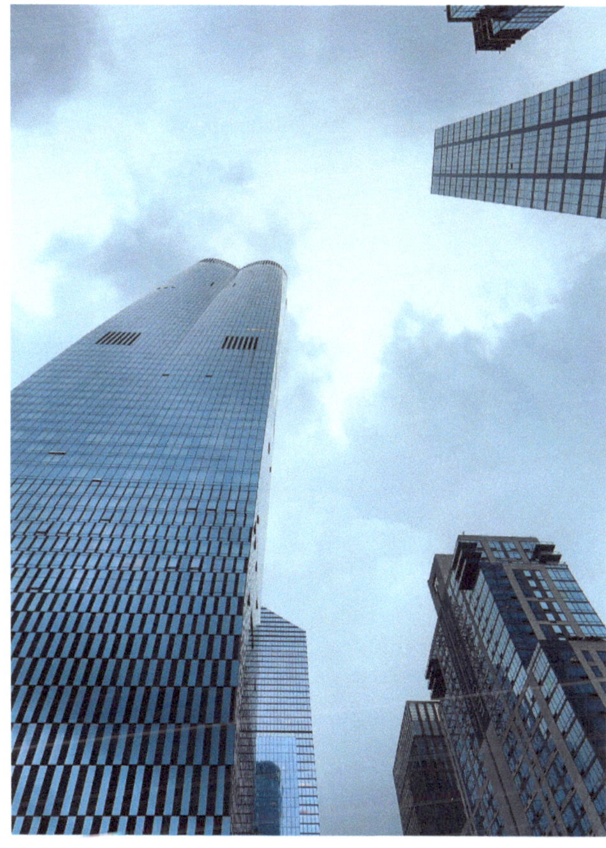

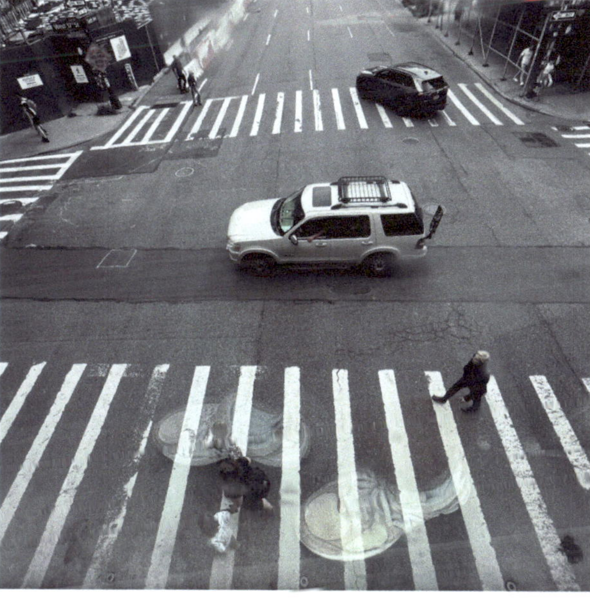

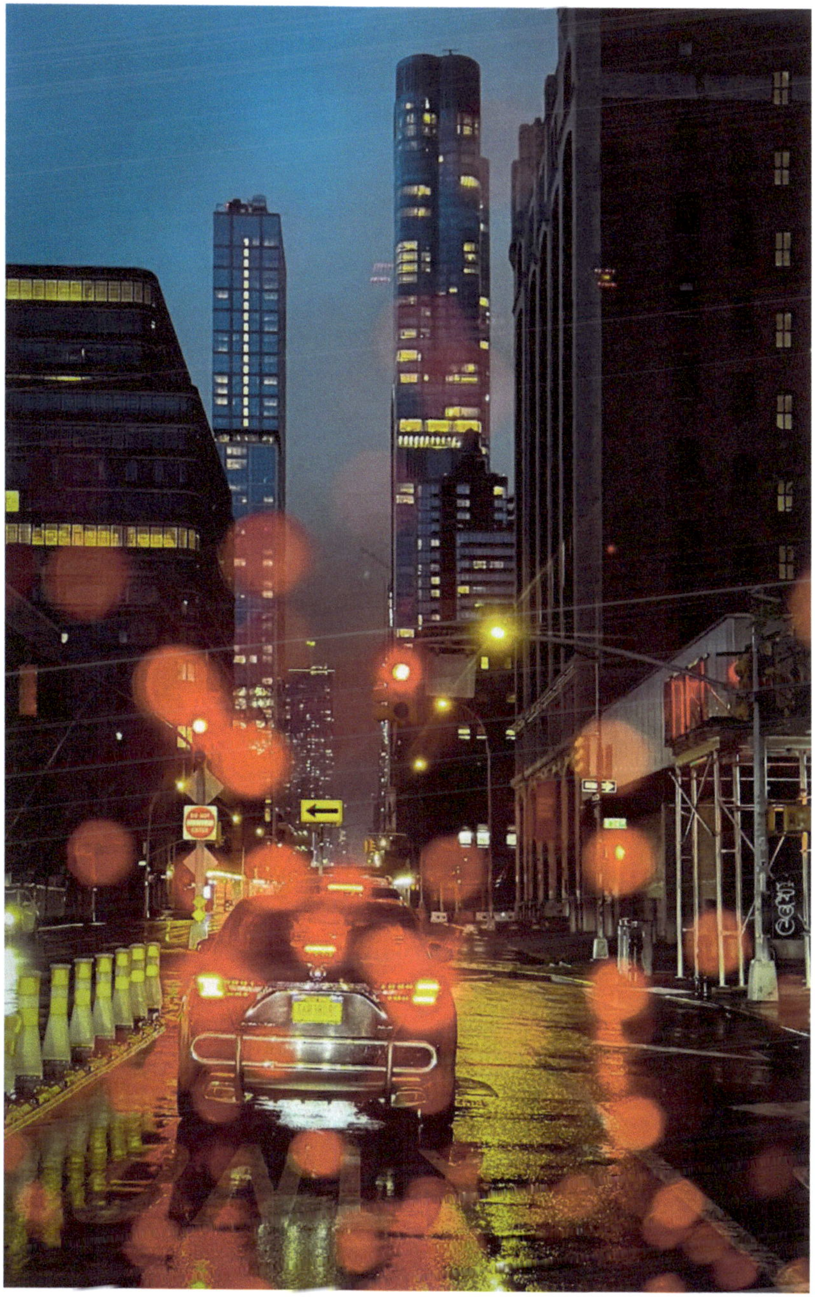

Crossroad

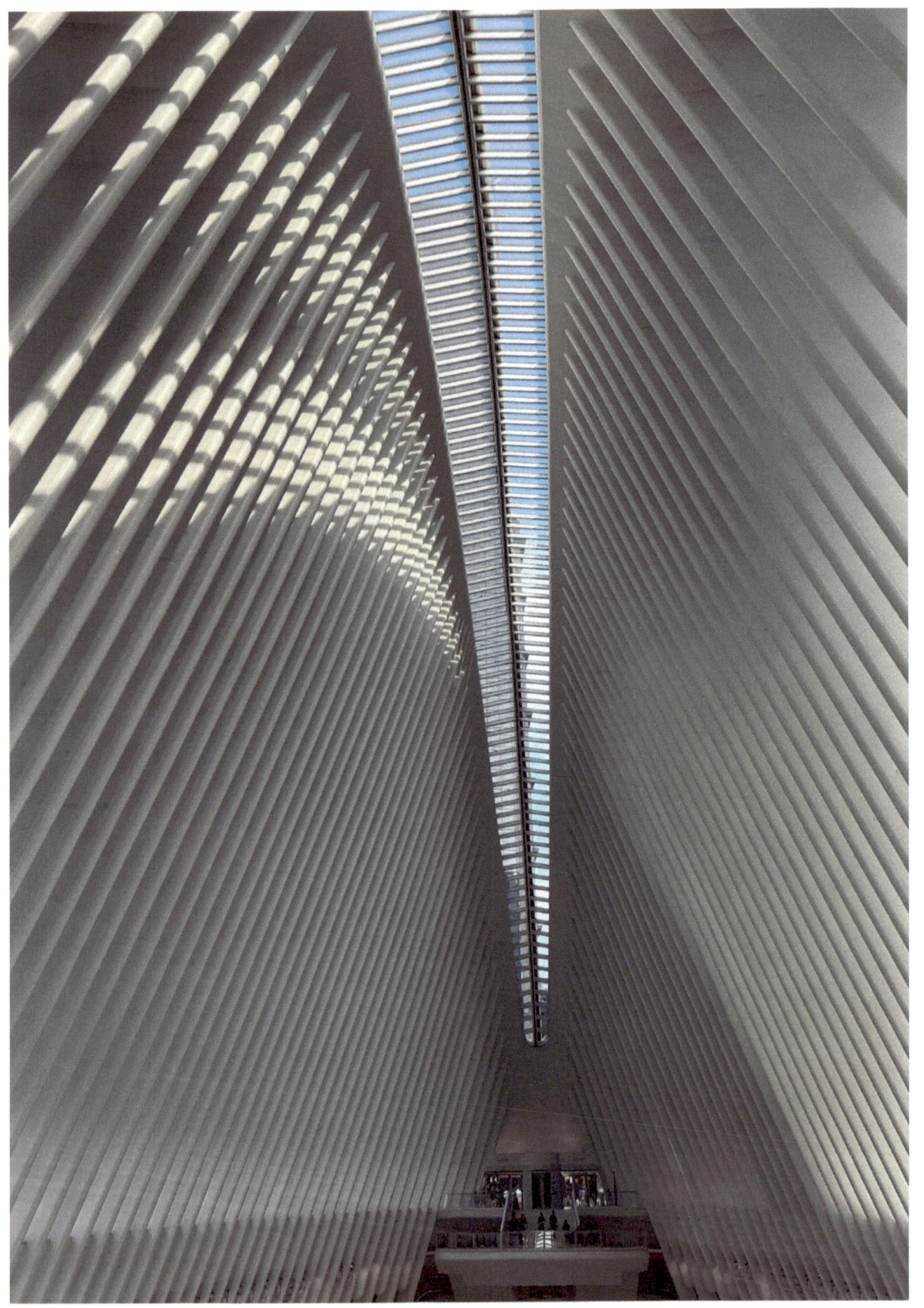

Soaring Spirit

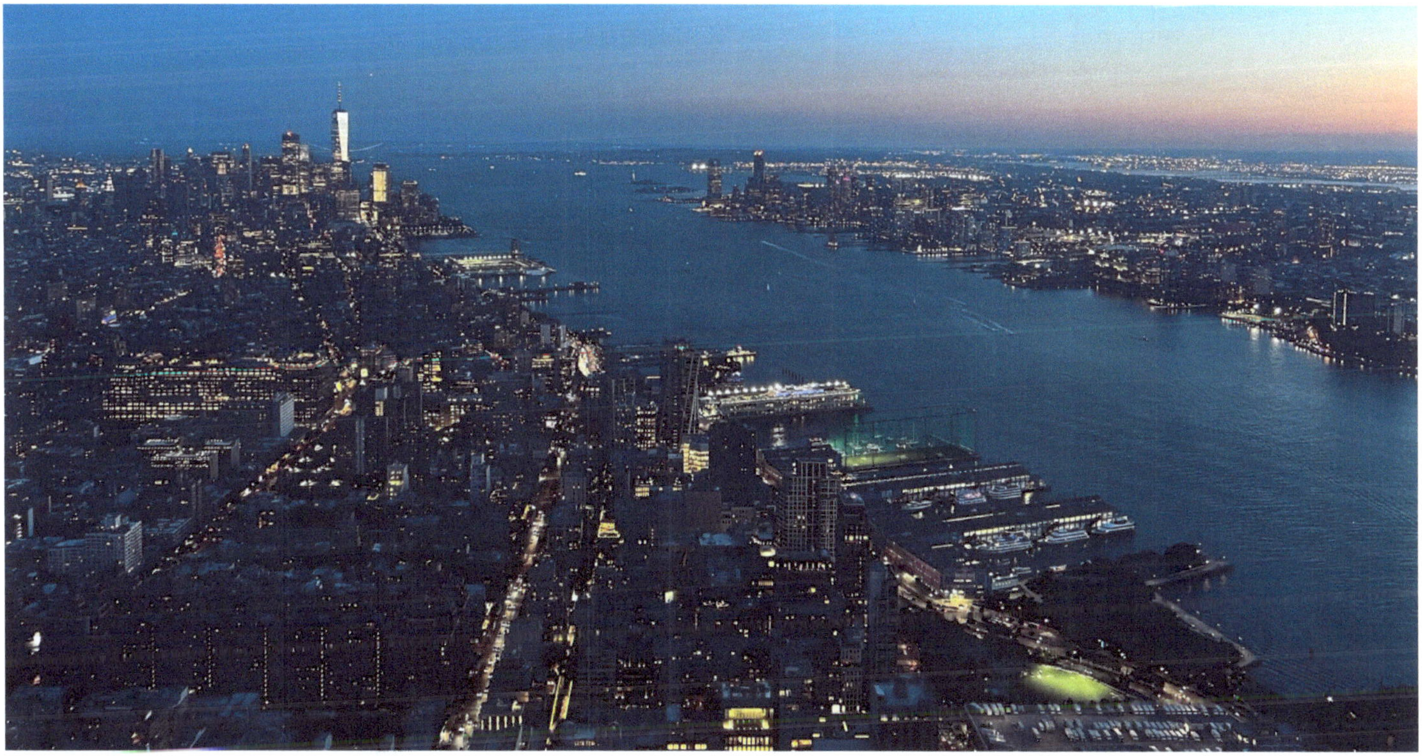

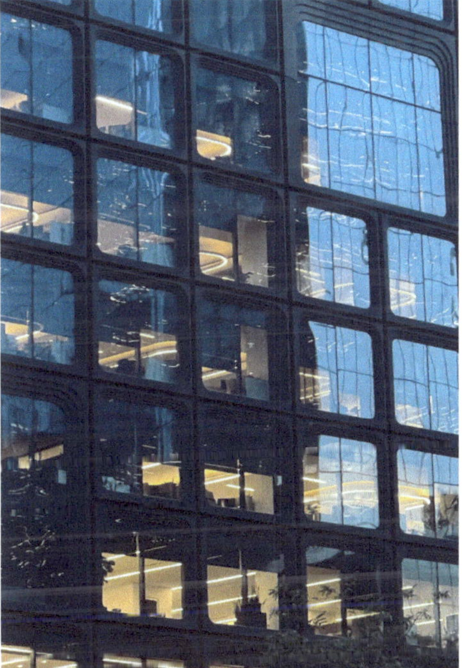

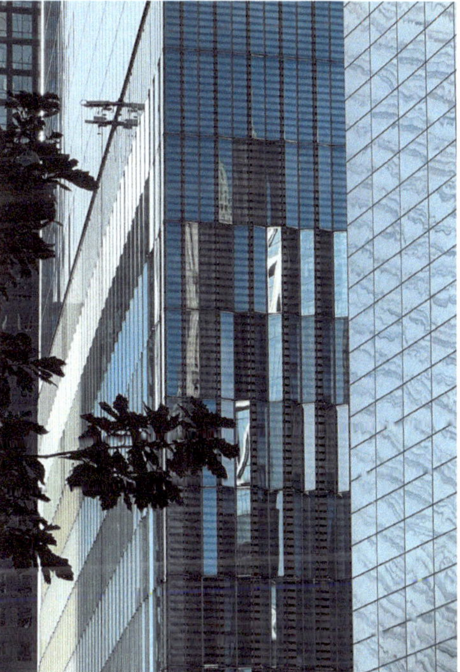

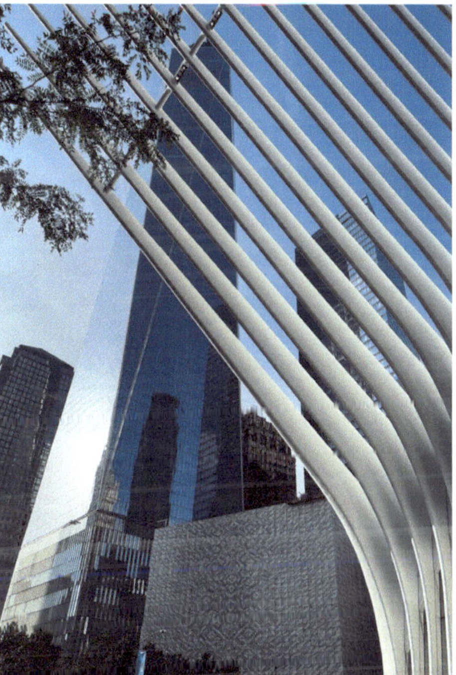

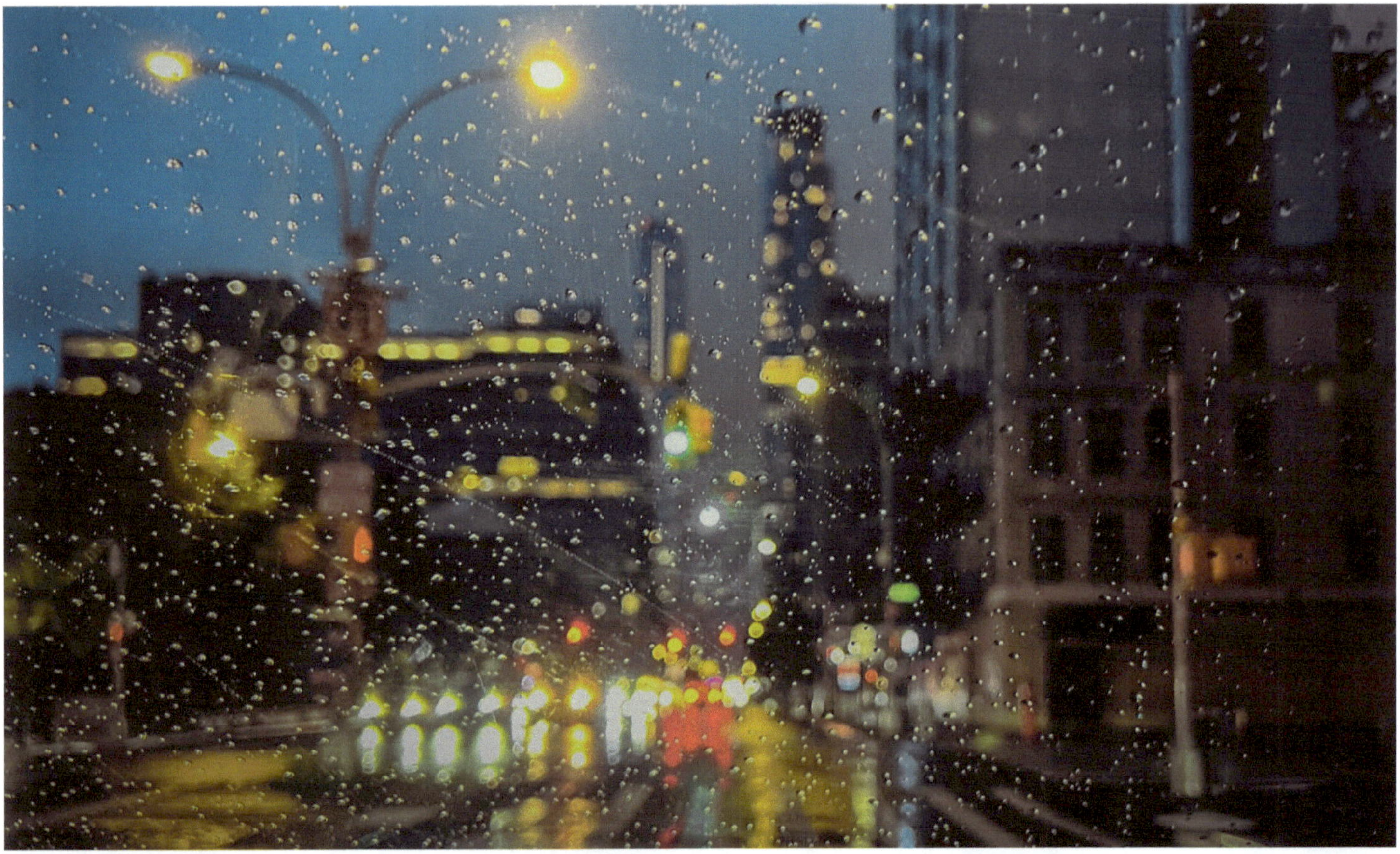

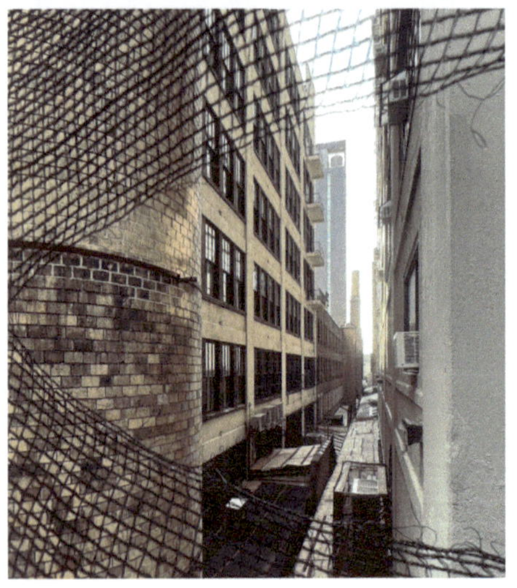

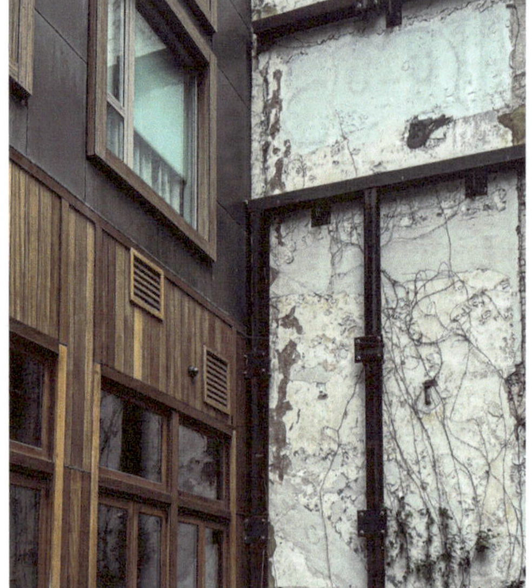

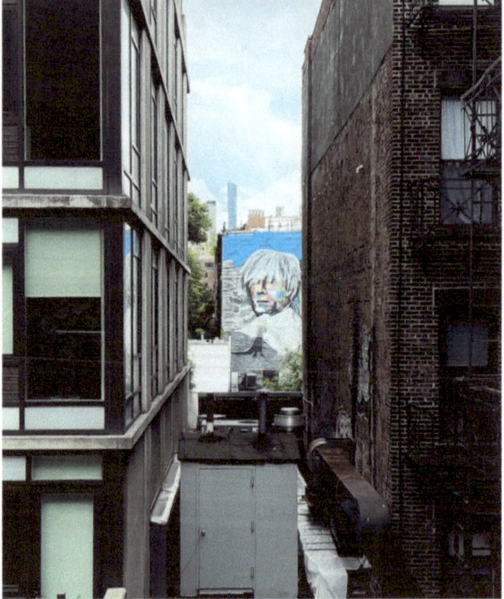

Cohesion

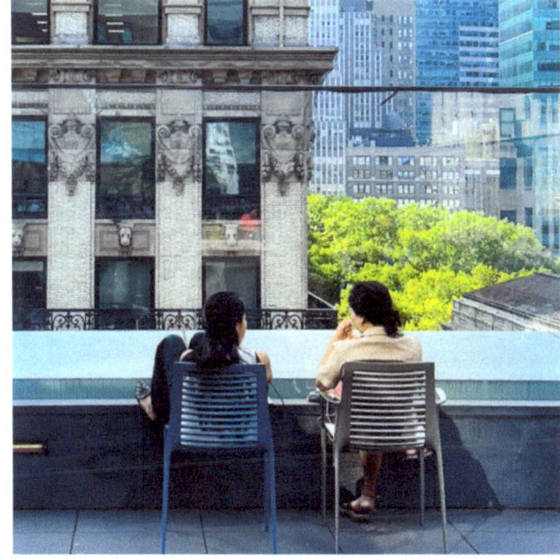

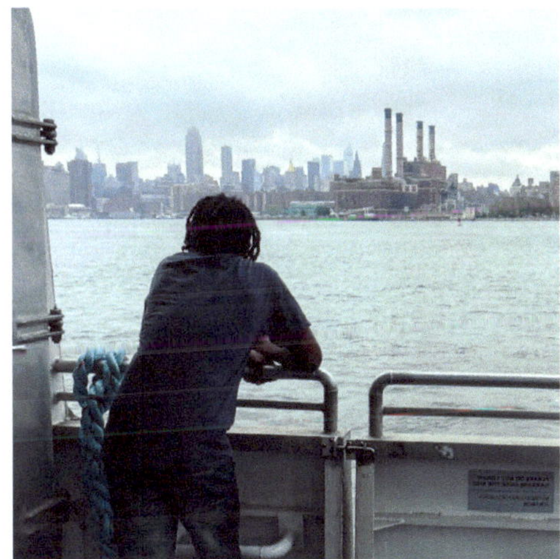

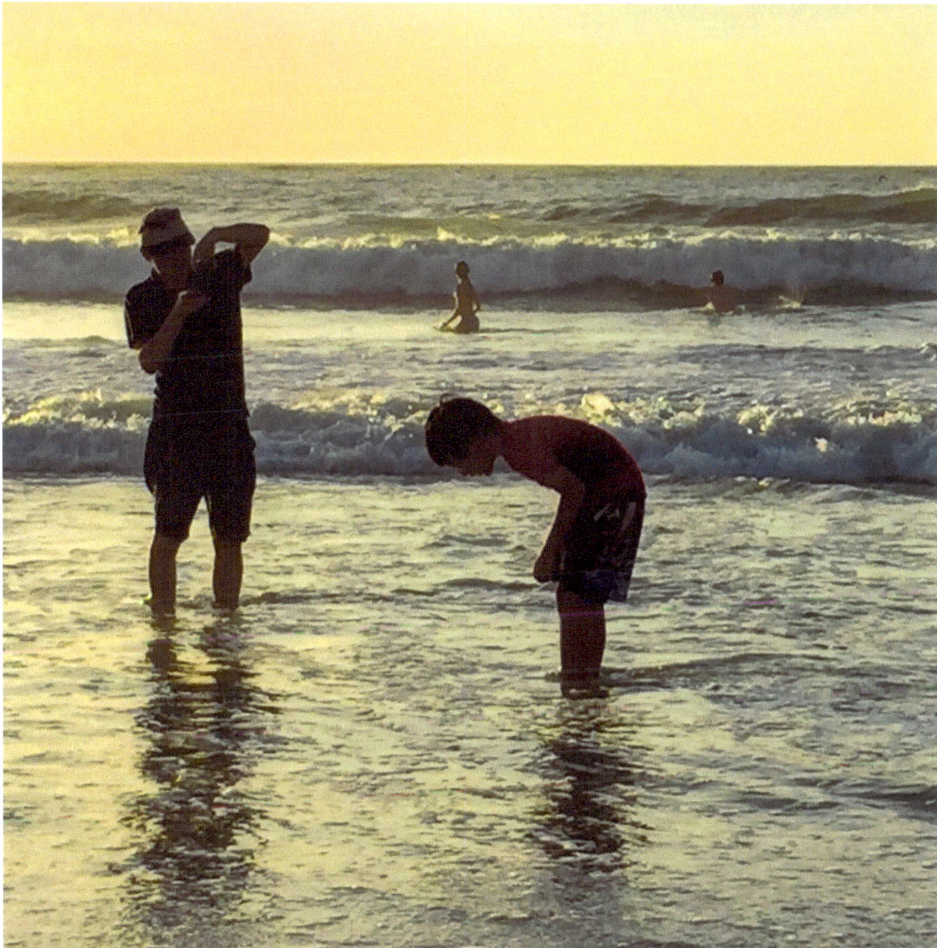

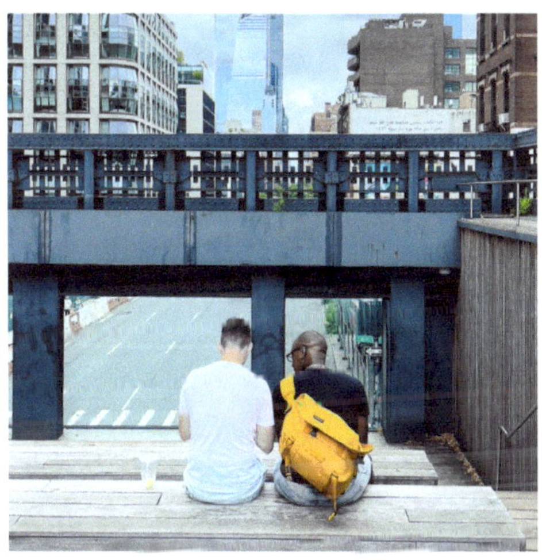

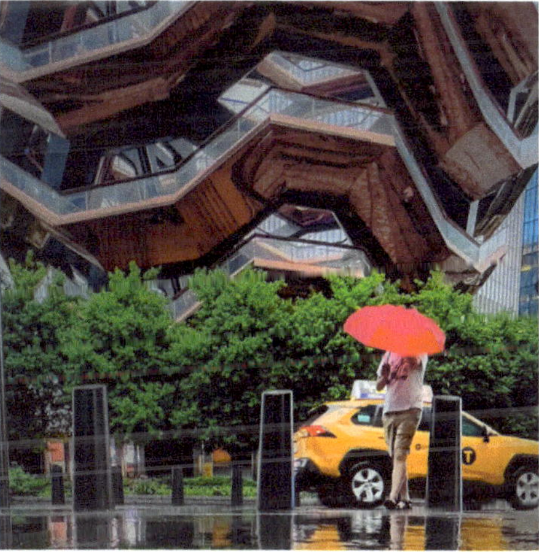

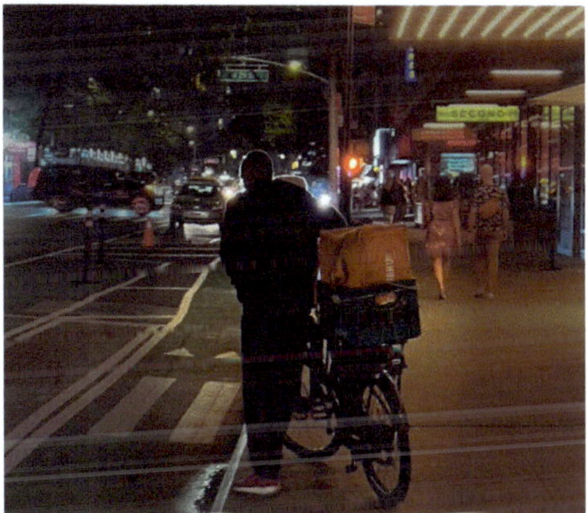

Moments

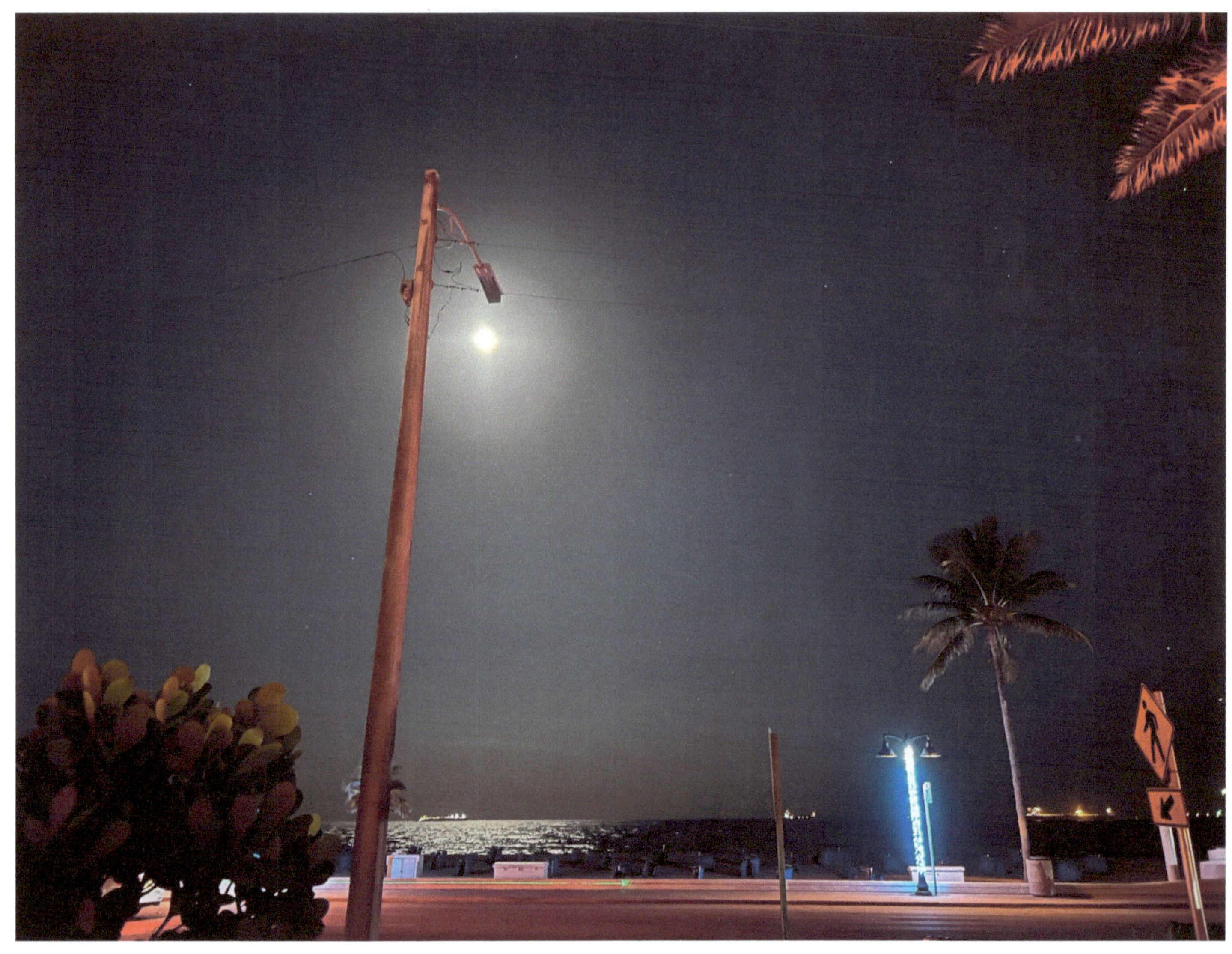

Midnight Sun   Seeing Blue

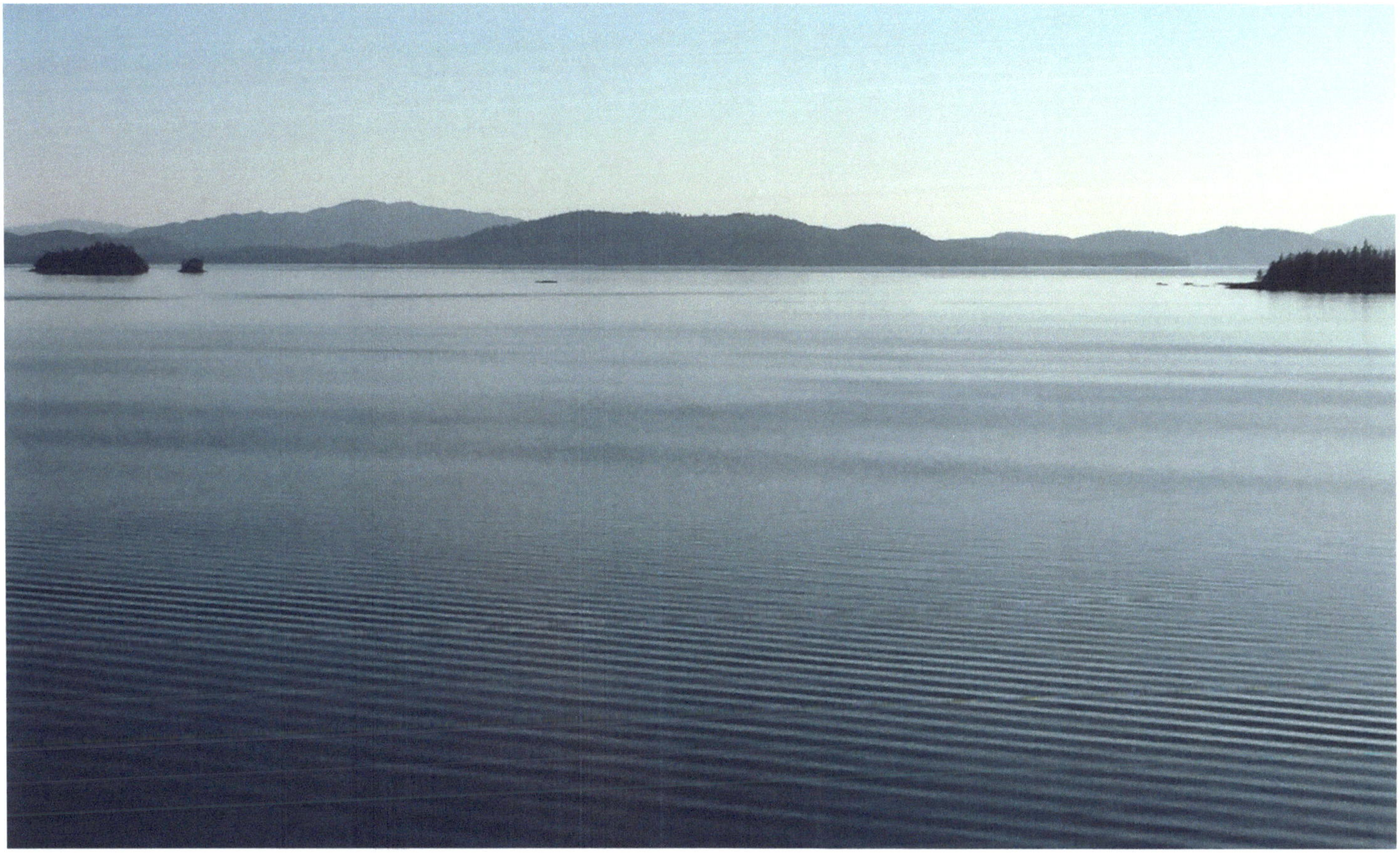

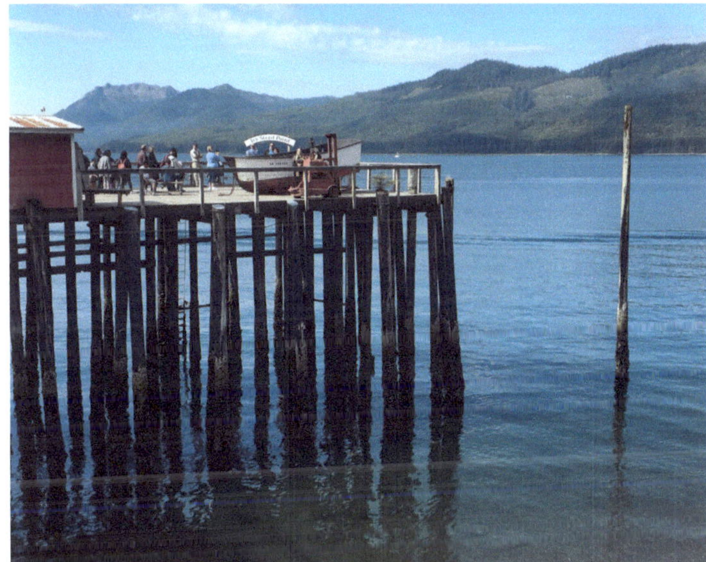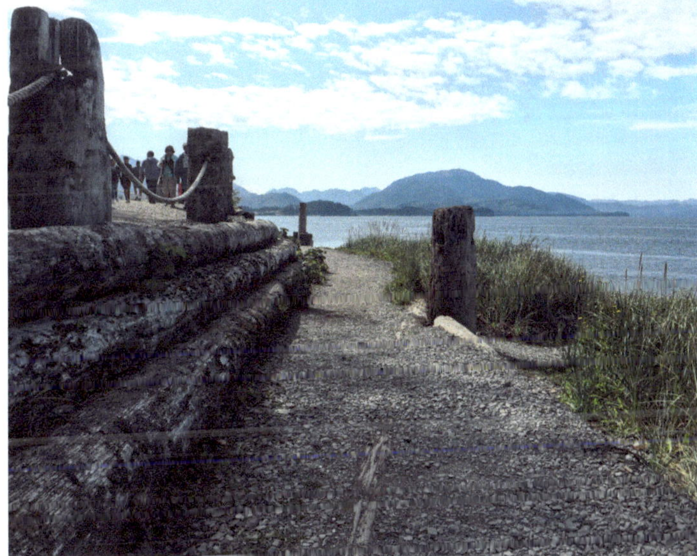

EXIT ONLY / DO NOT ENTER

ssical music
ents in
w York City."
York Classical Review
Tickets start at $20.
carnegiehall.org/
NYOInConcert
A Story
in Every

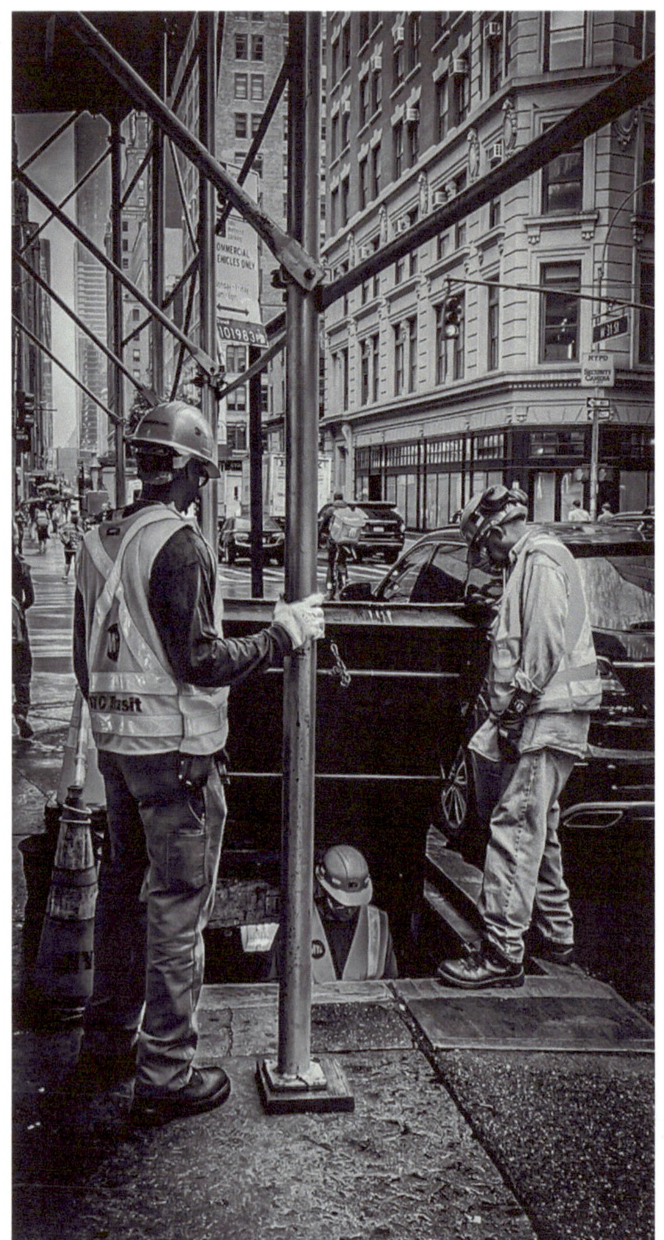

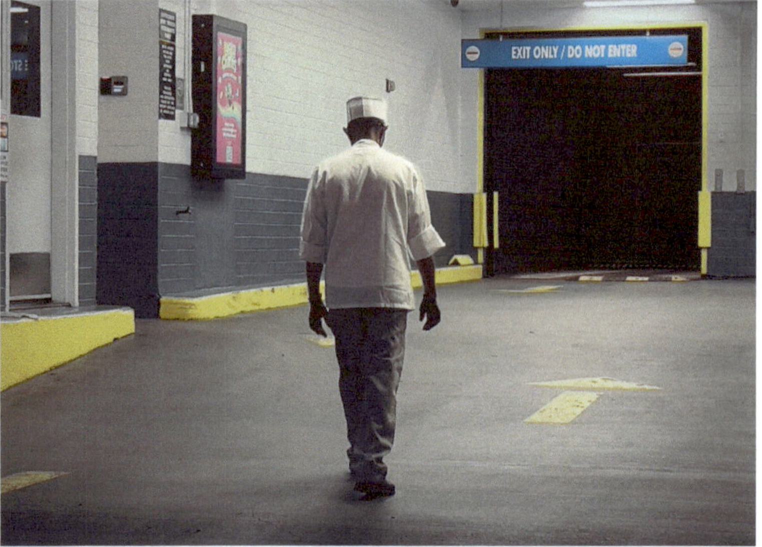

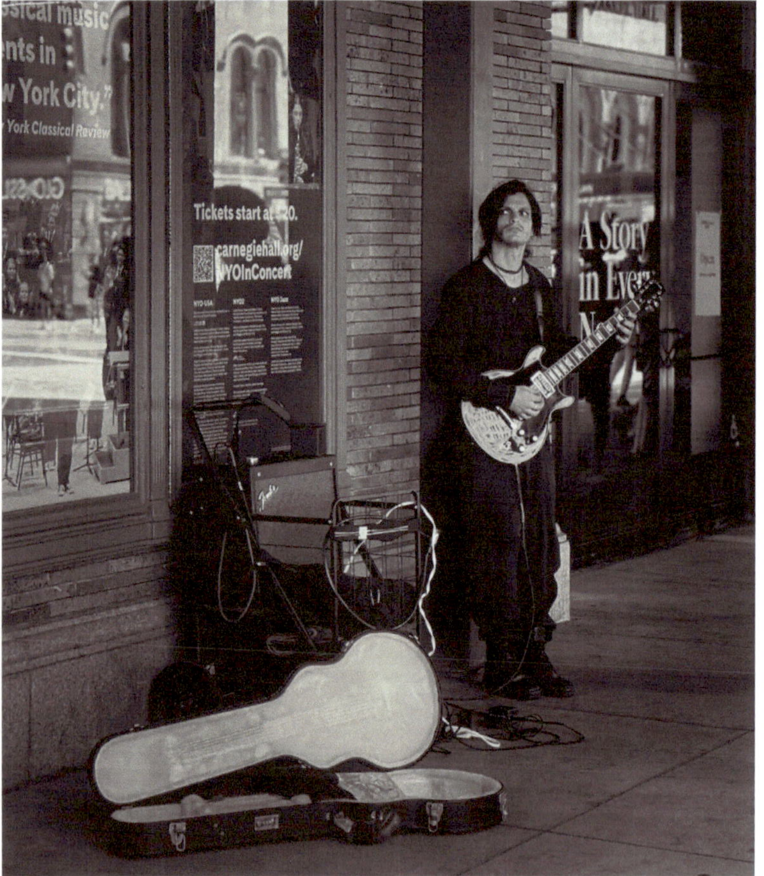

Grit

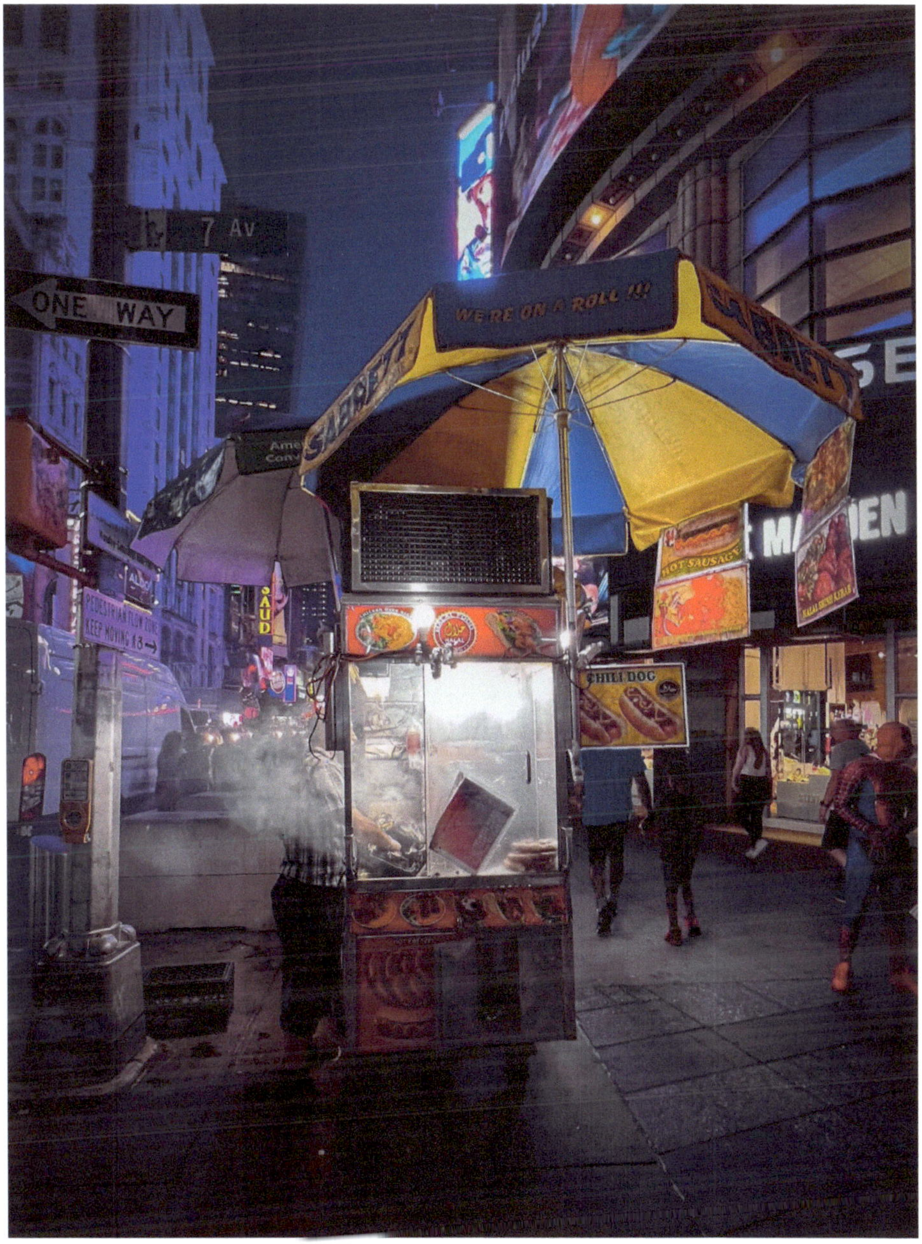

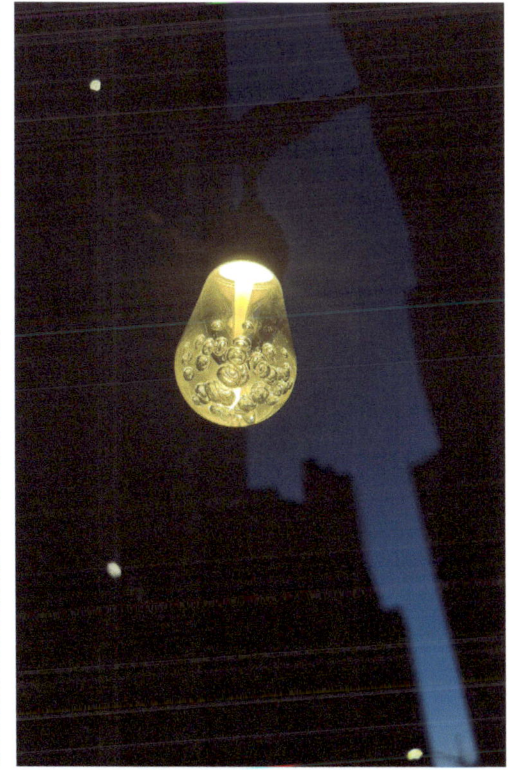
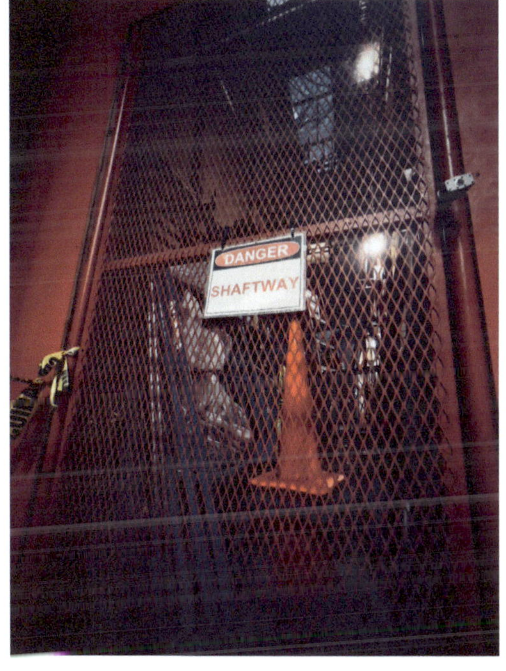

Hustle

ABOUT

Kai Zhou, a senior at The Westminster Schools
in Atlanta, is a budding urbanscape photogra-
pher.
With just his phone camera, Kai captures the
essence of the ordinary, offering a glimpse
into his perspective and the rich tapestry of
culture and history that is imbued in the plac-
es he photographs.

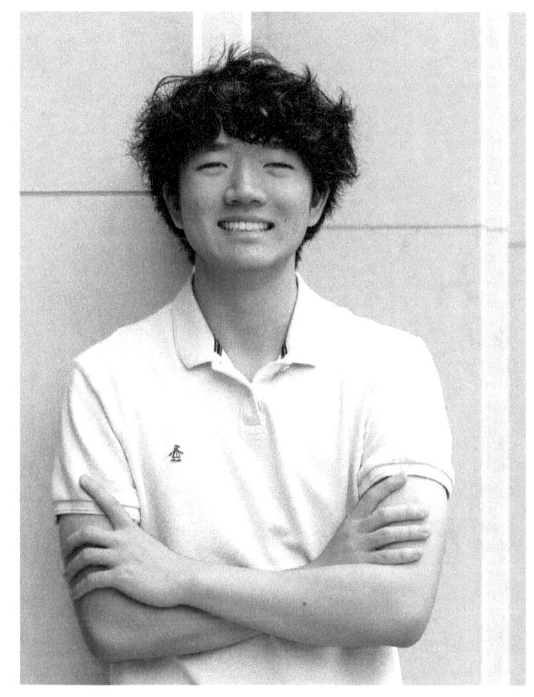